Laughter on the 23rd Floor

Laughter
on the
23rd
Floor

BY

Neil Simon

RANDOM HOUSE NEW YORK

TO SID CAESAR AND THE WRITERS:
MEL BROOKS, MEL TOLKIN, LARRY GELBART,
SHELDON KELLER, DANNY SIMON, GARY BELKIN, LUCILLE
KALLEN, SELMA DIAMOND, TONY WEBSTER, CARL REINER,
AND ALL THE OTHERS I'VE MISSED.

Laughter on the 23rd Floor *was first presented by Emanuel Azenberg at Duke University's R. J. Reynolds Industries Theatre in Durham, North Carolina, on October 19, 1993, and subsequently opened in New York City on November 22, 1993, at the Richard Rodgers Theatre, with the following cast:*

LUCAS	Stephen Mailer
MILT	Lewis J. Stadlen
VAL	Mark Linn-Baker
BRIAN	J. K. Simmons
KENNY	John Slattery
CAROL	Randy Graff
MAX PRINCE	Nathan Lane
HELEN	Bitty Schram
IRA	Ron Orbach

Jerry Zaks was the director. Scenery was designed by Tony Walton, the costumes by William Ivey Long, the lighting by Tharon Musser, and Steven Beckler was the production supervisor.

Act One

It is 1953.

We are in the offices of The Max Prince Show, *a television variety show. It is on the twenty-third floor of a building on 57th Street between Fifth and Sixth Avenues.*

This is the Writers' Room. It is actually two rooms made into one large room by breaking down the wall that separated them. We can still see where the molding has stopped between the two rooms.

The room is divided into two spaces. On Stage Left is where the actual writing takes place. There is a metal-top desk with a typewriter on it and a swivel chair behind it. A large leather sofa is to the left of the desk. On the opposite side of the desk and facing it, there is a large, comfortable sitting chair. This belongs to MAX PRINCE. *Around this grouping are chairs of assorted kinds, room enough for eight people to sit down.*

The other side of the room, at Stage Right, is more of a lounging area. There is a table against the wall with a coffeemaker on it, in which coffee is now perking. There are paper cups, and a few regular coffee mugs for the veteran writers. Also on the table is an assortment of fresh bagels, rolls, sliced pound cake, and Danish.

There is a small desk in this area with two chairs on either side and a telephone on top.

There is also a cork board on the wall to which index cards are tacked to denote the sketches that are being written. There are also piles of magazines, dictionaries, and thesauri about. There are two doors, one on each side of the room. Also, there are Emmys and other awards on shelves.

It is a few minutes before ten A.M. on a crisp Monday morning in March 1953.

AT RISE:

LUCAS BRICKMAN, *in his mid-twenties, sits at the center desk, writing. He looks up.*

LUCAS *(To the audience)* I guess this is what I've dreamed of my whole life. There was no comedy show in all of television that equaled *The Max Prince Show*. Not in 1953, there wasn't . . . *(He gets coffee)* An hour and a half revue every Saturday night, completely live. And now I was actually a writer on it. My name is Lucas Brickman. *(He sips coffee)* Max was unlike any comedian I had ever seen before. He didn't tell jokes. He didn't say funny lines. He was just funny. But on camera, when he had to be himself, like introducing a guest, he couldn't say four intelligent consecutive words without mumbling or coughing. I like Max a lot. Mostly because he treated his writers with respect. And he paid them more than anyone else. All young guys and they made more money than the governor of New York. Well, they were *funnier* than the governor of New York. *(He looks at his watch)* If I seem nervous to you, it's because it's only my second week here. One of the other writers left and I'm here on a four-week trial contract. So if I'm going to prove myself, I'm going to have to do it fast. My problem is, I'm shy . . . but I did manage to get one really funny line on last week's show. Unfortunately Max coughed on that line and no one in America heard it . . . My entire future depends on my finding a voice for my humor . . . or a cure for Max's cough.

(The door opens. MILT FIELDS, another writer, enters. He wears a black cape over a sports jacket, a bow tie, and a black beret on his head)

MILT *(In the doorway)* I did it. Broke every record on the Henry Hudson Parkway. Door to door, Scarsdale to Fifty-seventh Street, twenty-eight minutes, twelve seconds, made every light . . . Can you imagine if I had a car? *(Crossing the room to* LUCAS*)* Ba-dum-bum. How you doing, Arnie?

LUCAS Fine. It's Lucas.

MILT It's not Arnie?

LUCAS No.

MILT I called you Arnie all last week, you never said a word.

LUCAS I didn't know you were talking to me.

MILT You're going to have to learn to speak up, kid. Otherwise these killers'll eat you alive. *(He throws his cape)* Hang this up, willya? Be careful with it. It's an antique.

LUCAS *(He touches it)* Feels nice. Where'd you get it?

MILT I took it off a dead bullfighter in Spain. What do I know? A junk shop. But it's got style, class. I got a flair for dressing, no?

LUCAS A flair? You got a rocket. Where'd you get the beret?

MILT The beret is legitimate. Got it in Paris. The last one sold.

LUCAS The last beret in Paris?

MILT   MGM bought 'em all up for Gene Kelly movies. *(LUCAS nods)* Look, he believes me. What do I know about berets? And I look like a putz in this. So why would I wear it?

LUCAS   Why?

MILT   Because people notice it. Look at me without a beret. *(He takes it off)* Invisible, right? A nothing. Who is he? But watch. *(He puts the beret back on)* Now I'm someone. A diplomat. A traveler. Maybe I know Ernest Hemingway. I go to French movies, laugh at the jokes . . . *(He laughs)* don't understand a fucking word they're saying, but people come over on the way out. "You like the picture?" "Eh, comme ci, comme ca." I don't even understand *that* but I get attention. I'm unique, right?

LUCAS   Well . . .

MILT   What am I, good looking? No. Am I smart? Eh. Am I funny? Yes. But compared to the comic minds in this room, I'm Herbert Hoover's kitchen help . . . So I wear yellow suede shoes on Christmas and a cowboy hat on Yom Kipper. And when I walk in here, Max Prince laughs. And if Max Prince laughs, my kids eat this week.

LUCAS   Max didn't talk to me once last week.

MILT   Alright. I'll rent you the beret. Fifty bucks a week. If he picks up your option, seventy-five.

LUCAS   No, that's okay.

MILT *(He hands him the beret)*   Here. It's a gift. *(He pulls a red one from one pocket and a green one from the other pocket)* I'm up to my ass in berets.

LUCAS *(Smiles)*   And you don't think you're funny?

MILT *(Putting away the red and green berets)*   Cheap! Cheap laughs! These guys are Tiffany's. I'm a wholesaler. *(Crossing to the bagel table)* What they have in quality, I make up in quantity. Bulk, volume, that's my humor. Where's the onion rolls? It's in my contract. My agent negotiated for onion rolls.

LUCAS *(He points)*   Isn't that one?

MILT *(He picks up a small dark roll)*   This? This is a Jewish hockey puck. Smell it. Does that smell like an onion roll?

LUCAS   I can't smell. I have a cold. I could listen to it if you want.

MILT *(He grabs the beret from LUCAS)*   You're funny, Arnie. You're too quiet, but you're funny. Don't be *too* funny. I have a wife and two kids to support. It's murder on my mistress.

BOTH *(Together)*   Ba-dum-bum.

MILT   Yeah. You'll be alright.

(The door opens and VAL SKOLSKY enters in an old, worn topcoat over a somber suit and tie. He is the senior member of the staff. An emigrant from Russia when he was twelve, he still carries his accent. He is the most politically aware of all the writers)

VAL *(In a Russian accent)* Did Max get in yet? Excuse me. Am I interrupting? Forgive me. Pay no attention.

MILT The man apologizes three times in one sentence and hasn't said good morning yet.

VAL I'm sorry. Obsolutely unforgivable. I have a lot on my mind. It's an affliction common to geniuses. Just kidding.

   (He hangs up his topcoat)

MILT You like his coat, Luke? Val buys all his clothes at Ellis Island.

VAL Dot's right. Be funny before work starts. *(He rubs his hands, looks at food table)* So what have we got here? Nothing bot onion rolls. Ernie, do me a favor. Look for a pompernickel bagel.

MILT His name is Arnie.

LUCAS It's Lucas.

VAL It's not Ernie?

MILT It's not even Arnie . . . It's not even *pom* pernickel.

VAL Don't start with me. I didn't sleep last night. I didn't have breakfast. I didn't get laid in a week. And Max calls my house at twelve A.M. midnight. He never calls at twelve A.M. midnight unless there's trouble.

MILT Twelve A.M. *is* midnight, putz.

VAL Milt! Don't bother me. It's too early in the day to say go fock yourself.

MILT There's no such word as "fock." A person can't "fock" himself. You can't be a U.S. citizen until you say "Go *fuck* yourself."

VAL Kiss my naturalization papers, okay? *(Looks at buffet table)* I can't believe there's not one pompernickel bagel.

LUCAS *(He points)* There's one.

VAL *(He picks it up)* Thank you, Lukela. You'll go far on this show. *(He opens the already split bagel)* Look at this. Already sliced. *This* is why my father brought us to America.

LUCAS For sliced bagels?

MILT Mine came for chocolate pudding. In Poland they could make it but they couldn't get it in the cups.

VAL *(Putting cream cheese on his bagel)* I wonder if Max called anybody else last night? Did he call you, Lewis?

LUCAS Lucas. No. Why would he call me? Is anything wrong?

VAL I don't know yet. I was out last night. Oh, listen. I saw without doubt the most focking brilliant play I have ever seen in my life. I'll remember it as long as I live.

LUCAS What was it?

VAL What the hell was it? Downtown. In the Village. The Grapes Theater. Not the Grapes. The Peach. The Pear. The Plum. Whot sounds like that?

LUCAS The Cherry Lane?

VAL Dot's it. God bless you. You obsolutely get a raise this Christmas, we'll see, maybe, who knows?

MILT This is our head writer, Arnie. A man who learned to speak English from a dog who barked at night.

VAL Is dot right? I got news for you. My dog *dreams* funnier than you.

MILT My dog can say "fucking pumpernickel."

VAL Good. Then he can take your place on the show.

LUCAS So what was the play?

VAL What play?

LUCAS At the Cherry Lane.

VAL Ibsen. *Hedda Gobbler.*

MILT *Hedda Gobbler?* Is this about a turkey?

VAL You focking illiterate. I'll bet you five hundred dollars right now you don't know Henrik Ibsen's first name.

LUCAS You just said Henrik.

VAL I did? *(To* MILT) Alright. I'll bet you two-fifty. *(VAL laughs. To* LUCAS) Dot's funny. My mistakes are funnier than what he makes op. *(He looks at his watch)* It's after ten. Max is *never* this late. Now I'm worried.

LUCAS *(To* VAL) You don't have *any* idea why he called?

VAL *(Taking a sip of coffee)* None. He spoke to my maid. In Swedish. Double-talk Swedish. To a woman who's here three weeks from Peru. She was still crying when we came home . . . Something's op. I swear to God.

MILT *(He speaks into the phone)* Honey, can I have an outside line, please?

VAL God daddammit, you know the rules, Milt. Is this a business call or a personal call?

MILT I don't know. Let's see who answers.

LUCAS It seems incredible, growing up in Russia, that you became a comedy writer. I mean, did they have television there?

VAL Television? They don't have doorbells yet. *(To* LUCAS) And yet the greatest comedy in the world came from Russia. Gogol, Chekhov, Dostoevsky. The best. Read *Dead Souls* sometime. Absolute genius. But in Russia today, comedy is dead. Lenin killed it. Stalin buried it. And what have they got now? The most corrupt and insidiously evil political regime since Ivan the son of a bitch . . . No, sir. Until there are humane reforms in that country, I wash my tongue of their language. *Ptui! (He spits out)* I'm sorry. I got cream cheese on you. Totally unforgivable.

MILT *(Into the phone)* Hello? Who's this? . . . No, I'm calling Collette.

VAL Collect? We've got a show to write and you're calling some girl collect?

MILT *(To VAL)* *Collette!* Her name is Collette, not "collect." Why don't you go to Berlitz and drive *them* crazy?

VAL Hey! This is not a day to get me angry, Milt, I swear to God.

MILT Alright, put me down for Wednesday. *(Into the phone)* Yes, I'm holding.

VAL *(He looks at his watch)* Where is everyone? Five after ten and we haven't put two lousy words down on paper.

MILT He's right. Hey, Luke. Put two lousy words down on paper. *(He speaks into the phone)* Collette? Milt. Listen, babe. We'll have to cancel tonight. It's my wife's birthday. Unless I can convince her she's wrong.

(The door opens and BRIAN DOYLE *enters, a lit cigarette in his mouth. He wears a rumpled dark tweed jacket with baggy pants. He is starting to get bald but he has newly made dots on his scalp from a recent hair transplant. He is Irish, about twenty-nine, a heavy smoker, a heavy cougher, and a heavy drinker, but with a biting sense of humor as caustic as his outlook on life)*

VAL   Brian! Jesus! You picked a bad time to come late.

BRIAN   I'm sorry. I just stopped to—*(He coughs)* I stopped to—*(He coughs again, almost uncontrollably, then stops)* I stopped to get some cigarettes.

  (He hangs up his coat)

LUCAS *(To the audience)*   Brian Doyle. Good guy, good writer, lousy smoker.

MILT   Hey, guys. Please. I'm cheating on the phone here and I can't hear a goddamn thing.

VAL   That's it, dammit! Dot's a fifty-dollar fine.

MILT   I gotta go, honey. They just raised the rates. I'll call you. *(He hangs up)* Oh, Brian's smiling. Something happened. He met someone at the convent.

BRIAN   Five days! Count 'em, guys, that's all you get. Because on Friday this good-lookin' Irishman is leaving the show. The Gentile makes good.

LUCAS   Where you going?

BRIAN   I think they call it—Hollywood? Sold my screenplay to Metro. MGM? You must have heard of it.

LUCAS   MGM? That's *great!*

VAL   Every week he's leaving the show on Friday. Every week he's flying to Hollywood. Every week he sold a screenplay to MGM or Twentieth Century–Fox.

MILT   Not Fox. *Fucks!* I keep telling you.

(BRIAN hums "I'm Singing in the Rain")

VAL   That's it! I want a sketch started immediately right now before Max gets here. Who knows what shape he'll be in? Lucas, get *Newsweek, Time, Life,* every magazine. See what's in the news. Milt, see what ideas we got on the board. See what's a hit picture. Maybe there's a Marlo Brandon movie Max can do.

(MILT takes idea board off the wall)

LUCAS   Marlon Brando.

VAL   What did I say?

LUCAS   Marlo Brandon.

VAL   My way was funnier. *(BRIAN has pulled a piece of cake off with his fingers)* Hey, Brian. When you're through destroying the pound cake, maybe you'll find time to come up with an idea.

BRIAN *(To LUCAS)*   Come here, Luke. These guys still don't believe me. *(BRIAN takes out a small piece of paper. He hands it to LUCAS. LUCAS looks at it)* That's history, kid. Right up there with David Selznick buying *Gone with the Wind.* Go on. Read it.

LUCAS *(He reads the small note paper)*   "Your agent called and said MGM will get back to you."

(LUCAS, MILT and VAL look at each other)

VAL   . . . Go on. We're listening.

LUCAS   That's it.

MILT   That's it? "MGM will get back to you" is a deal? . . .

BRIAN   I got a call from the coast last night. They sign the contract soon as they okay the script.

LUCAS   They didn't okay it yet?

BRIAN   They'll okay it as soon as they read it.

LUCAS   They didn't read it yet?

BRIAN   They'll read it when I write it.

MILT   *You didn't write it yet?*

BRIAN   *(He points to his head with index finger)*   Here! It's all up here! Every page, every word, every comma.

VAL   They made a deal for your finger pointing to your head?

BRIAN   You jealous bastards. I told the idea to my agent, my agent told it to MGM. The whole studio is crazy about it. You see these guys, Luke? Thirty years from now they'll be writing game shows and I'll be V.P. of MGM screwing Lana Turner.

MILT   When she's sixty-two? Why?

VAL   I categorically resent your remarks. Dis is, without a doubt, the finest writing staff in the history of television. And I would rather stay here till my prostate falls out before I ever sold out to the dreck and garbage of Hollywood. God's truth, even if they asked me.

BRIAN   What if they asked you?

VAL   I'm open to everything. You can tell them.

> (KENNY FRANKS *walks in. Neatly dressed, sports jacket, tie, raincoat, tortoise-shell-framed glasses. He is surely the most sophisticated of the lot)*

KENNY *(Holding up* Time *magazine)*   Did you see this? This week's *Time* magazine? Pope Pius approves of psychoanalysis . . . This means from now on confession will be eighty bucks an hour . . .

LUCAS *(To the audience)*   Kenny Franks, boy genius. They say he was writing jokes for Jack Benny when he was fourteen. I wasn't allowed to stay *up* for Jack Benny when I was fourteen.

VAL *(He looks at the* Time *magazine that* KENNY *put on the desk)*   You think maybe this Pope thing would make a sketch for us?

KENNY   Well, I think we'd all have to take Communion first.

BRIAN   Take it. It beats circumcision.

> (KENNY *pours hot water into a mug, puts tea bag in it, then lets it cool)*

MILT *(To* BRIAN*)*   What the hell would a Gentile like you know about circumcision? *(To others)* Did you ever see him in the men's room? He pisses straight up the wall. *(*KENNY *takes a pill with a cup of water)* So, Mr. Vitamin, what kind of pill are we taking today?

KENNY   Nicotine tablets. *(He drinks it down)* Now I can get cancer without having to smoke. *(*BRIAN *laughs.* KENNY *stirs his tea)* How you doing, Luke?

LUCAS   I don't know. Nobody tells me.

KENNY   Don't worry. Max thinks you're going to be great.

LUCAS   Did he say so?

KENNY   No, but I'll tell him he did. He doesn't remember.

(He sips his tea)

VAL *(To* KENNY*)*   Did you hear about Max calling me at twelve A.M. midnight?

KENNY   Did you know he called *me* at eleven-thirty?

VAL   *Max* did?

KENNY   He was sitting in his den, piss drunk, with a loaded shotgun on his lap.

VAL   Son of a bitch. He told you this?

KENNY   Well, it sort of dribbled out of his mouth, but I got most of it.

VAL   Son of a bitch.

LUCAS   He had a loaded gun?

KENNY   He said he got another threatening letter in his mailbox last night.

MILT   It wasn't me. I sent my letter last week.

VAL   Son of a bitch. Did he call the police?

KENNY   Well, he said he was taking the matter in his own hands. It's him against them now.

BRIAN   Son of a bitch. Sorry, Val. There was one open.

VAL *(To* KENNY*)*   What do you mean, him against them? Who's them? Did he say?

KENNY   The man was on tranquilizers and scotch. Every time he talked he blew bubbles.

LUCAS   Tranquilizers?

MILT *(To* LUCAS*)*   Max gets in his limo every night, after work, takes two tranquilizers the size of hand grenades and washes it down with a ladle full of scotch. His driver helps him into his house and he falls asleep on the floor of his den next to his dogs.

BRIAN   Exactly. That's why there are no letters. The man is paranoid.

VAL   Maybe Brian's right. Remember when Max accused his next-door neighbor of shooting up the tires on his Cadillac?

BRIAN   Hey, guys. Max shoots up the tires himself. We all know that.

LUCAS Why would he do that?

BRIAN He has a gun. He has a Cadillac. He's free on Sundays. Why not?

LUCAS Does Max have any enemies?

KENNY Beside himself, I don't think so.

LUCAS What do you mean?

KENNY Nobody hates Max the way Max hates Max.

BRIAN I love it when you talk like Gertrude Stein.

KENNY *(To* LUCAS*)* They don't get it. We *write* comedy. Max *does* comedy. It's his ass out there in front of the cameras every week.

MILT Is that his ass? No wonder he gets such big laughs.

VAL No. Kenny's right. Max likes it in here, with us, not out there. The funniest man since Chaplin and he still throws up before every show.

BRIAN For twenty-five grand a week, I'd put my fingers down my throat.

MILT Hey, Brian. Don't ever knock Max in this room. He puts bread on my kids' plate and he's transplanted every hair on your head.

(He takes BRIAN*'s cap off, revealing transplants)*

BRIAN *(He touches his hair)* If I didn't tell you, you'd never know.

KENNY   So what are the dots on your head for? Tick-tacktoe?

MILT   I hear transplants grow in like pubic hair. That means you'll have to get a zipper for your face.

BRIAN   Gee, I'm really going to miss you guys in Holly-wood.

(*The others react*)

KENNY   Oh, Jeez. He sold another script? What putz studio bought it this time?

LUCAS   MGM.

KENNY   For how much?

BRIAN   Seventy-five grand.

KENNY   No, I mean how much you want to bet you're full of shit?

BRIAN   Name your price.

KENNY   Five hundred bucks if you win. If you lose, we all get to pull out your transplants . . .

(CAROL WYMAN *enters, carrying a shoulder bag. She's about twenty-eight, with a strong and quick defense system that comes with being the only female writer on the staff*)

CAROL (*Excited*)   Have you guys heard the news? (*They just stare at her*) . . . Of course not. No one else here cares about what's going on in this country. Am I the only one here who takes an interest in something besides jokes and cars and money and baseball?

ALL except VAL *(They look at each other and nod)* Yeah, you're the only one . . . Right . . . You got it . . . You do it, we're busy.

VAL What's the news?

CAROL I just heard it in the taxi. Joe McCarthy called General George Marshall a Communist.

VAL Un-focking-believable.

CAROL He calls a five-star general of the army a card-carrying Communist.

BRIAN Even if he *was* a Communist, why would he have cards printed up?

CAROL Hey, children. Wake up. Time for school . . . You think this is a joke? America's on the brink of becoming a fascist state and this doesn't worry you?

BRIAN McCarthy's a nut case. A drunken fanatic. How long you think he's going to last?

VAL Some of them lasted long enough to kill six million Jews.

BRIAN Hey, I met hotheads like McCarthy. He'll start a fight in an Irish bar one night and get a dart right between the eyes.

CAROL   I feel so badly for General Marshall. Such a nice man. Such a sweet face. Of all names to pick, why him?

MILT   I don't know. Val, did you ever see Marshall at any of the meetings?

VAL   *Are you out of your focking mind?* You don't make jokes like dot. Some secretary outside hears dot and the next thing I'm being subpoenaed in Washington.

CAROL   Val is right. No Communist jokes. None of us are safe today. *(She whispers)* They got that blacklist thing, you know.

MILT   They got what?

CAROL   *(She whispers)*   Blacklist. Blacklist.

KENNY   Three bags full.

CAROL   Don't you guys realize they can put anyone— *(She whispers)* on the blacklist they want.

LUCAS   Without proof?

KENNY   In a second. They've got a wait list to get on the blacklist.

MILT   Not if you tip the maitre d'.

CAROL   I can't believe they think this is funny. Did any of you see Edward R. Murrow last night?

MILT   I don't live in his neighborhood.

CAROL   What do I have to do to impress you this is serious?

MILT   Well, the whispering was good.

CAROL   Two top U.S. senators told Murrow the FBI were tapping their phones.

VAL   You see? Same as Russia. First the politicians, then they go after the arts. The writers first because they're the intellectuals.

BRIAN   Well, this room looks pretty safe.

CAROL   You think so? Whoever has access to the public is McCarthy's enemy. That's us. *(Whispers)* I bet they have a bug in this room right now.

MILT   Well, you leave crumbs, you're gonna have bugs. *(VAL glares at him)* It was a political joke. I thought you'd like it.

KENNY   . . . Don't you see, you're playing right into McCarthy's hands. Fear through intimidation.

MILT   He doesn't intimidate you? A United States senator who giggles like Porky the Pig?

VAL   My God, this is a terrible time for all of us.

BRIAN *(Looks at his watch)*   Twenty after ten, he's right.

CAROL   Oh, my God. Oh, no.

VAL   *What?*

CAROL   I have a cousin. My mother's nephew. A nice, sweet, stupid boy. He was a Communist in college for three months, then he quit. What would I do if they asked me about him?

VAL   You take the Fifth Amendment.

MILT   Or the Sixth Avenue subway. You get off in China.

KENNY   Okay, guys. Enough. We're heading into the Cancer Zone of humor.

CAROL   You know how Max hates McCarthy. Wait'll he hears about this.

BRIAN   Wait'll you hear about Max.

CAROL   What?

LUCAS   He got a threatening letter.

CAROL   From McCarthy?

BRIAN   No. He writes them himself.

VAL   You don't know that.

KENNY *(To* CAROL*)*   He called me last night. Had one of his scotch-tranquilizer combos. Sitting there with a loaded shotgun on his lap.

VAL   Said he was going to shoot the bastards.

CAROL   Hasn't he got those two hunting dogs? Maybe that's all it is. He was just going to go hunting.

KENNY Those dogs don't hunt. They point to food in supermarkets.

VAL Okay, God forgive me for mentioning this word . . . Nervous breakdown.

MILT That's two words. God'll never forgive you.

KENNY Wait a minute. Let's not go off half cocked . . . First one who makes a joke on that is in trouble.

MILT Listen, if you're half cocked, you're in *enough* trouble.

(MILT *looks at* VAL, *then* KENNY, *then takes a sip of coffee*)

KENNY Has Max ever missed a show? Has Max ever missed a rehearsal? Has Max ever missed a writing session? Never. He's in this room with us every day. Never an ego-inflated shit like most of the comics we've all worked with. Max is a professional. He's dependable. He's reliable. He's eccentric but he's not crazy.

VAL Then why, for the first time, is he a half hour late?

KENNY He probably stopped to shoot his dogs, his toes, and his tires. But he'll be here.

(*The phone rings*)

VAL If that's bad news about Max, I don't want to hear it.

MILT   Whoever wants to hear bad news about Max, pick up the phone.

(*It rings again*)

VAL   Godammit, someone pick op the phone.

LUCAS *(Farthest from phone)*   I'll do it.

BRIAN   He's just a kid. What does he know about picking up a phone?

CAROL *(She picks up the phone)*   Hello? ... Oh. Hi. Where are you? *(Covering mouthpiece)* It's Ira. He's running late at his analyst's.

MILT   I thought his analyst died.

CAROL   He met another one at the funeral. *(Into the phone)* Ira, just get here, we have problems. *(She hangs up)*

LUCAS *(To the audience)*   Ira Stone was a hypochondriac who came in late every day with a new ailment. His greatest wish in life was to have a virus named after him. *(The phone rings again)* Can I get this one? I think I'm old enough now. *(He picks up the phone)* Hello? ... Oh. Okay. Thanks, Helen. *(He hangs up quickly)* Max just walked in. He stopped off in the john.

VAL *(Nervously)*   Alright. Everybody calm down. Relax. What do we say to him?

CAROL   Do we mention anything about the letters or the loaded shotgun?

LUCAS   He must know because he told Kenny last night.

VAL   We should make a quick decision what we say. How long you think he's going to pee in there?

BRIAN   My friend had a German shepherd who flew from Paris to New York. When he landed, he peed for two hours and ten minutes.

LUCAS   Can you imagine what Lindbergh must have done?

VAL   You know what? I don't want the responsibility of being head writer anymore. I swear to God. I quit. Carol, you're head writer.

CAROL   I'm trying to get pregnant. I have enough to worry about.

BRIAN   Ask your husband. Why should *we* do everything?

(*The door opens.* MAX PRINCE *enters. He is in his early thirties. He wears a trench coat over a gray double-breasted suit, black shoes, a white shirt, and a tie. He appears to be taller than he is because he exudes great strength. His strength comes more from his anger than from his physique. He dominates a room with his personality. You must watch him because he's like a truck you can't get out of the way of. He is quixotic, changing quickly from warm, infectious laughter to sullen anger. He is often monosyllabic, offering a word or two to convey his thoughts. Today is not a good day for* MAX. *He storms across the room almost oblivious to them*)

VAL   Oh, just talking about you, Max. We were saying the response to Saturday's show was unbelievably good. Maybe the best ever.

CAROL   I got at least twenty phone calls.

MILT   I made ten myself, that's how good it was.

MAX *(He paces angrily)*   Any reports on the show?

VAL *(A little bewildered)*   Yes, Max. Unbelievably good. Maybe the best ever.

MAX *(Still pacing)*   What did they say?

VAL   . . . They said unbelievably good. Maybe the best ever.

MAX   Mug.

> *(He hangs up his trench coat)*

LUCAS   What?

MAX   Mug.

VAL *(To LUCAS)*   Mug. He wants coffee in his mug. No cream, four sugars.

LUCAS   Oh right, Max.

> *(He quickly goes to get the coffee)*

MAX   Did we get any more memos from NBC?

VAL   What?

MAX   Memos! Memos! They love to send memos.

VAL   No, Max. No memos.

MAX *(He mocks acting hurt)*   No memos? They skipped a day without memos? They're saving them so they can memo me to death. They'll bury me in a folded memo in the Mount Memo Cemetery in Memo Park, New Jersey.

LUCAS *(He comes back with coffee)*   Here's your coffee, Max. Be careful. It's very hot.

MAX *(Takes the cup and then drinks it all down without stopping)*   *Whoooooooh . . .* that was hot.

VAL   You shouldn't drink hot things so fast, Max.

MAX   No. It's good. Boils the blood.

CAROL   You want an aspirin, Max?

MAX   Took a bottle at home.

BRIAN   Well, a bottle of aspirin should clear it up.

CAROL   Did you get any sleep last night, Max?

MAX   Oh, yeah. Slept like a bear.

KENNY   Those bear sleeps are great, heh, Max? You wake up in April, May, you feel like a million.

(MAX laughs and unzips his pants, taking them off over his shoes. Holding his pants and jacket, he crosses to the door and yells out)

29

MAX   HELEN! I'M READY!!

HELEN *(from offstage)*   Coming, Max.

MAX *(To others)*   We work today. Lotsa work. I want to do a great show this week. *No!!* Not a great show. The best. Best show we ever did, you hear?

MILT   Sure, Max. It's always good to change it once in a while.

> (MAX *is standing in his shirt, shorts, socks, shoes, and garters.* HELEN *enters. She is an attractive secretary, in her late twenties.* MAX *hands her his jacket and pants)*

MAX   Dry cleaned and pressed.

HELEN   Like always, Max.

MAX   And check my pockets. I don't want my keys pressed.

HELEN   Yes, Max. Oh, Mr. Revere of NBC sent you a big pile of memos.

> (MAX *looks furiously at the others.* HELEN *leaves with his suit and closes the door.* MAX *crosses to his rack, gets his trench coat, and puts it on)*

MAX   Ohhhhkay! . . . They started, we'll finish. You all heard it. NBC fired the first shot. Remember this day, everyone. A day that will live in infamy . . . March sixth, 1953.

BRIAN   . . . It's March eighth, Max.

MAX *(He glares at him)* What are you, a historian?
. . . March sixth, March eighth, March twelfth, who
gives a damn? . . . *(He sits, lights his cigar)* The battle
has started. The lines have been drawn. Now we have
to plan our counterattack.

CAROL *(To* KENNY*)* What's it about?

KENNY *(He shrugs, then turns to* MAX*)* What's up, Max?

MAX What's up? What's not down is up . . . What's up
could be down, what's down could be up. You understand?

KENNY Certainly. It's Newton's Theory of Obscurity,
isn't it?

MAX *(He lights his cigar)* They want to cut the show
down to an hour.

CAROL An *hour*?

VAL Us? We're number one show in the country.
Maybe two, three the worst.

MAX Cutting us down. Right at the kneecaps. Chop
chop chop chop chop.

KENNY Can't you reason with these people, Max?

MAX What people? NBC is not a people. They're not
like us. They wear black socks up to their necks. Crew-
neck socks . . . They come home from work and before
dinner, they dance with their wives . . . They put up
wallpaper in their garages . . . You can't talk to them.

KENNY   Then what is it they want?

MAX   Alright. *(He holds up his cigar)* . . . What is this I'm smoking?

(They all look at each other)

BRIAN   I'll take a chance, guys . . . *(To MAX)* A cigar?

MAX   Wrong.

BRIAN   Damn. I thought I had it.

MAX *(To BRIAN)*   To *us* it's a cigar. To them it's power. To them it's control. To them it's grabbing our testicles and *squeezing* them. *(He grabs them and squeezes, grimacing in pain.* MAX *then turns to* CAROL *and squeezes his testicles)* You understand?

(LUCAS and MILT look toward CAROL)

MILT *(As an aside to CAROL)*   I'll explain what that feels like later.

VAL   Forgive me, Max. I don't mean to interrupt. Let me see if I can understand . . . The cigar is a phallic symbol, i.e., the penis . . . i.e., the penis is power, i.e., the penis is control. Right?

MAX *(Nods)*   I ee I ee oh!

KENNY   So NBC is using their power to control us, right, Max? To do what?

MAX   To cut out my *heart!* They want to cut the budget, save money. He says the show is too sophisticated. Too smart, he says. My own sister, my own brother, two people who never graduated from *spelling,* understand every word. The big money sponsors want out, he says. What do they sell? Raisins? Macaroni? Cream cheese? People who eat and chew can't understand this program? . . . Who does he think we're playing for, dogs and cats?

CAROL Can they just say that, Max? "From now on you've got an hour and that's it"?

MAX They can say what they want. They can sit in their offices with their camel-hair carpeting, hitting golf balls into their toilet bowls . . . eating their little salmon ball wedgies for lunch . . . Let 'em. But I've got a plan.

CAROL What's the plan, Max?

MAX Okay. Close the doors.

LUCAS *(He looks)* The doors are closed, Max.

(MAX *leans forward in his chair. Motions to them to lean in. They all do)*

MAX When the Thracians fought the battle of the Modena Heights in 354 B.C., outnumbered by a hundred thousand men, what did Cyclantis, the greatest military mind in all of history, decide to do?

(They all look at each other again)

MILT *(To* CAROL*)* Was Cyclantis the giant with the big eyes?

33

VAL   Will you let the man finish? . . . What did Cyclantis do, Max?

MAX   He sent out one hundred women, old, young, whatever . . . placed them ten miles apart in a—in a—

   (He makes a circle with his finger)

KENNY   A circle?

MAX *(He nods)*   A circle . . . covering two hundred miles. Then in the dead of night, each of the hundred women lit a—lit a—

   (MAX *makes an upward hand gesture)*

VAL   An umbrella?

MAX   A *torch*. Big torches . . . An umbrella? The enemy saw the torches all around them, thought they were surrounded, threw down their arms and sounded surrender. Y'hear? The surrounded sounded surrender . . . and that's what we're going to do.

MILT   Get a hundred women with torches and surround Rockefeller Center? *(VAL glares at him)* I'm just asking. I was never *in* the army.

BRIAN   I say we just kill the fuckers.

MAX   You got it.

KENNY   Can you tell us *exactly* what NBC did, Max?

MAX   They sent me their Declaration of War. In the mail. Delivered to the house where my wife and children sleep. There's going to be blood spilled. Oh, yes. But not in my house. Their palaces will crumble and their kings will fall and their wheat fields will be scorched.

MILT (*As an aside to* CAROL) NBC has wheat fields?

KENNY Let me ask you, Max. Is it NBC who's been sending you the threatening letters?

MAX Who told you about that?

KENNY You did. Last night. You called me, remember?

MAX I called *you*?

KENNY Yes.

MAX Last night?

KENNY Right.

MAX That was you?

KENNY I swear.

MAX It didn't sound like you.

KENNY I tried my best, Max.

MAX You sounded foreign to me. Spanish maybe.

VAL That was my maid from Peru.

MAX She was at Kenny's house?

VAL   No. In *my* house. You called me after you called Kenny.

MAX   I never spoke to you.

VAL   No. I was at the theater.

MAX   I called you at the theater?

VAL   No. You called me at my house. I went to the theater. In the Village. The Peach. The Pear. The Plum.

LUCAS   The Cherry Lane.

VAL   The Cherry Lane. Thank you.

MAX *(To* LUCAS*)*   You were with Val?

LUCAS   No. I was at home. With my wife.

MAX   I called you at home?

LUCAS   No. Not me. Val wanted to know what theater he went to and I told him.

MAX   Val called you to ask what theater he was in?

LUCAS   No. He already came home. He asked me this morning.

MAX   I didn't even know you were married.

LUCAS   Well, this is the first time we ever talked.

36

MAX *(He holds his head)*   I can't remember anything. I think somebody's drugging me, I swear to God.

VAL   Well, Max, that brings up another delicate subject.

MAX   I fell asleep the other night with my eyes open. I thought I was dreaming about a ceiling.

VAL   In the first place, Max, you know we all love you.

MAX   Sometimes I go in the kitchen in the middle of the night, get a hammer and smash walnuts. Why would I do that?

KENNY   I think Freud says that's a symptom of fear.

MAX   Why? I'm not afraid of walnuts . . . You want to hear the worst part?

CAROL   I thought we did, Max.

MAX   When I eat, I can't tell the difference between steak and fish anymore. Why is that?

(He is near tears)

BRIAN   Where did they catch your steak, Max?

(MAX *glares at* BRIAN. BRIAN *looks away)*

MAX *(To* VAL)   What was the delicate subject?

VAL   Well, it's just that we feel for your own good, Max, for your own health, for your family's well-being . . .

MAX   I don't want to hear my fortune. I just want to hear the delicate subject.

KENNY   We don't think those pills you take before you leave here at night are good for you, Max.

MAX   *(Confused)*   What pills?

VAL   The pills, Max. That you take before you go home.

MAX   I take pills? What are you talking about? Those tranquilizers? They're prescription. Two little pills.

KENNY   *Little* pills? We could play nine innings of softball with one pill.

MAX   I hardly take them. Once a week.

BRIAN   You take them once a week every night, Max.

MAX   They're harmless. Carol, remember you weren't feeling well one night? I gave you half a pill. Did anything happen?

CAROL   I don't remember. I slept for nine days.

KENNY   It's not just the pills. It's the four jiggers of scotch you take to wash them down. Pills and liquor don't mix, Max. Or max, Mix, however you want.

MAX   I gotta sleep. If I don't sleep, who's gonna protect my family from them?

CAROL   NBC is threatening your family?

MAX   They're threatening my show. My show is my life. If they threaten my life, they threaten my family. You want to hear the letter they sent me? You want to know what they said, word for word for word?

MILT   Go ahead, Max. The doors are still closed.

MAX   *(He leans back in his chair, then looks at his cigar)* . . . They said . . . "Give the people shit."

(They all look at each other)

CAROL   The president of NBC said that?

MAX   You heard me. "Give the people shit."

BRIAN   You mean as a gift?

CAROL   Why would he say that, Max?

MAX   Because—they can make money on shit. A pot full. Drive up to Connecticut, they got big Tudor shit houses wherever you look, that's why they invented television. They put shit on for people to watch, they advertise shit, the people run out and buy the shit, their kids break the shit, so they buy them more shit and the shit moguls go to France in the summer and the poor people stay here and watch more shit . . . That's why I got a letter saying, "Give the people shit."

MILT   *(As an aside to CAROL)*   Isn't that what Marie Antoinette said?

CAROL   *(Swatting MILT)*   Why do you always talk to *me*? Annoy somebody else once in awhile.

39

KENNY   Let me take a whack at this. For four years in a row we sweep the Emmy Awards. Every critic in the country loves us. But suddenly television is expanding. They're going into the Midwest, the South. Different kinds of audience. They want to watch quiz shows, bowling, wrestling, am I right?

MAX   *(He nods)*   If you got shit, shovel it over.

KENNY   So they want to cut us to an hour. Don't make the shows too esoteric. Too smart. Don't do takeoffs on Japanese movies, Italian movies.

MAX   Feed a horse hay, what are you going to get?

CAROL   You don't even have to say it, Max.

KENNY   So it's not only cutting the half hour, it's the kind of show they want us to do.

VAL   Can't we talk to them, Max?

MAX   Talk? No! No talk! Fight! We fight them on the sea, we fight them on the beaches. Or we'll get the bastards in an alley in Brooklyn somewhere. Remember what Churchill said? "Never have so many given so much for so long for so little for so few for so seldom."

> *(He nods to the others . . . then* MAX *crosses to the coffee table and pours water into a paper cup. He carries it back, then sips it)*

CAROL   My God! This ties up with everything that's going on in this country today. The censorship. The blacklisting. It's Senator McCarthy publicly disgracing a man like General George Marshall.

MAX *(Spitting out water)* *What??* What did he say about Marshall?

CAROL You didn't hear? It was on the radio all morning.

MAX *(He crushes the paper cup. Water erupts)* What'd he say? I want to hear it exactly. Say it slowly, I don't want to miss a word.

(MAX *crosses to his chair. He takes a final sip from his crushed cup and puts it on the coffee table)*

CAROL Joe McCarthy accused General George Marshall, a five-star general of the army, of being a member of the Communist Party.

(MAX *squeezes the arm of his chair so tightly a piece breaks off. He gets up, so angry we can see the veins in his neck)*

MILT *(As an aside)* Somebody trade places with me.

(MAX *moves around, seething)*

VAL We know how you feel, Max. We feel the same way.

MAX You feel the same way I do? . . . I don't think so. Would you like to know how I feel? Ask me. Ask me how I feel about McCarthy.

CAROL Don't ask him, Val. I'm afraid to see.

MAX You don't want to see, don't look. *(To* VAL*)* Ask me how I feel.

VAL We can already *see* how you feel, Max.

MAX *(To* VAL*)* Not yet. When you ask me, then you'll see . . . *Ask me!*

> (MAX's *hand beckons strongly to be asked.* KENNY, *who sits between* MAX *and* VAL, *turns slowly to* VAL)

VAL How do you feel about McCarthy, Max?

MAX Thank you. *(He turns and smashes his fist through the wall. His hand remains in the hole. It's the wall that had the sketch ideas before* MILT *took them down)* There! That's how I feel.

CAROL Oh, my God!

VAL Are you alright, Max?

BRIAN Someone go in the other room and see how McCarthy is.

MAX They want me to give them shit? There! I gave them shit.

VAL Can you get your hand out, Max?

MAX *Leave it there!* Get a knife. Cut it off. Send it in a box to that no-good bastard. Let him know what I think of him.

CAROL Someone get his hand out. It could be broken.

(MAX *pulls it out. It is still in a fist*)

MAX *(He calls out)* HELEN! GET IN HERE! *(To* CAROL*)* Called him a Communist, heh? *(He looks around)* I want to hit something. Something big. Something expensive.

MILT There's a bank across the street, Max.

(HELEN *rushes in*)

HELEN Yes, Max?

MAX *(He points)* You see this hole? Don't touch it. Leave it there. Call up a framer. No. Call Tiffany's. I want that hole framed in their *best* silver. And underneath I want a plaque. Gold! And on the plaque I want engraved, "In honor of General George Marshall, soldier, statesman, slandered by that son of a bitch, McCarthy."

(HELEN *writes this down*)

HELEN I'm not sure that Tiffany's will print that, Max.

MAX You pay 'em enough, they'll print it.

HELEN Yes, Max.

(She rushes out. BRIAN, *who had left the room, sticks his head through the hole in the wall)*

BRIAN I think this could be a national monument. Like Monticello.

MAX *(An idea hits him)* *Okay! Okay, I got the sketch for this week's show!*

KENNY   What is it, Max?

MAX   I want to be the Statue of Liberty. I want to wear a long gown down to my toes.

VAL   I like that.

MAX   With big sandals. And a tiara. With a torch and a book. I want to be painted green. With bird shit on my shoulders from the pigeons. And I'm standing on this box that says, "Give me your poor, your hungry, your sunburned, your toothless" . . . whatever they got there.

MILT   We'll look it up.

VAL   Goddammit, dot's funny, Max.

KENNY   And what happens?

MAX   She gets subpoenaed. To Washington. She comes in the courtroom, the bottom of her dress is dripping wet from the harbor. With codfish in her hair.

(He "squeezes" water out of imaginary bottom of dress)

LUCAS   This is terrific.

MAX   And he's sitting up there looking at her. Senator Joseph McNutcake.

KENNY   *McNutcake?* . . . We can't say that, Max. Not on the air.

MAX   You don't think it's funny?

44

KENNY Yes, it's funny. I don't think eight years in jail would be funny. You can't say McNutcake.

MAX *(He thinks)* How about McBirdbrain? . . . McFruithead? . . . McFahrblungett. It means "crazy" in Yiddish, he'll never understand it.

VAL Someone'll tell him.

MAX So we do nothing? Is that what you all want to do? Nothing?

MILT I don't think having a long life is nothing, Max.

MAX Where I grew up, we took care of bullies. There was a big fat shlub in my class. We called him Tank Ass. He used to steal my sister's lunch. One day I put a rock in her sandwich. That taught him.

CAROL He bit into it?

MAX He ate it. The whole rock. He had to start wearing iron underwear. We gotta do *something,* guys.

VAL We feel the same as you, Max.

MAX No, you don't, you don't know how I feel.

MILT *(To VAL)* Don't ask him. It'll look like Swiss cheese in here.

MAX I'm not lying down. I'm not doing nothing. We gotta make some kind of stand, like Spartacus in the war against the Byzantimums.

VAL So what do you suggest we do, Max?

45

MAX   We quit. We tell them to keep their show and put on shit seven days a week. We walk out of here in single file, our hands up in the air like the heroes of Bataan . . . We're off the air as of today. No show Saturday! . . . That's what Patrick Henry said.

VAL   He said "no show Saturday"?

(MAX *glares at him*)

KENNY   If we walk, Max, they'll sue us.

MAX   Listen, are we together or not? Because if someone here doesn't want to quit, I don't want him here. He can leave.

MILT   That'll show him, Max.

MAX   I'm calling them now. *(He crosses to phone)* I'm telling them our decision is immediate, unanimous and conclusionary. *(He picks up the phone)* Helen, get me NBC. *(He speaks with his hand over the mouthpiece)* I just want to know if we're agreed.

VAL   Is it possible to talk first, Max?

MAX   Yes, it's possible but it's not gonna happen. Listen, we have to stick together on this. Otherwise I'm going to ask everyone to leave the room and I'll have a closed vote. You'll vote yes, then it's closed.

MILT   Think of it this way, Max. If we go off the air, isn't there a good chance they'll find someone *else* who doesn't mind giving them shit?

MAX   Someone else's shit isn't mine . . . Do you know who said that?

CAROL   Tell us, Max. We'll get it wrong.

MAX   It's in the Bible. You have to look for it.

BRIAN   "Someone else's shit isn't mine" is in the Bible, Max? Where?

MAX   Bottom of page one sixty-two. You think I memorized the whole Bible, for crise sakes?

KENNY   Max, it's a dumb idea. You've worked your whole life for this show. You think ABC or CBS are any different? They have corporate minds, Max. If they could get a TV set to turn out sausages, we'd all be pigs instead of writers. They're not interested in culture. Maybe if Van Gogh and Goya were wrestlers, they'd put them on Friday nights. But if we quit, Max, they win. We give up an hour and a half to *Miss America* and *Beat the Clock* . . . We stay, Max. We do what we've been doing for years. Only we do it better. And we keep doing it. And you know why, Max? Because maybe we'll never have this much fun again in our entire lives.

(*There is silence.* MAX *hangs up the phone and sits*)

MAX   . . . I served under General Marshall in the war. We were together in the European front.

MILT   I thought you were in the navy, Max. Playing in a band.

MAX *(He slowly turns to look at* MILT*)* . . . He came to a dance I played in London. He was fox-trotting ten feet away from me. I played a saxophone solo in his honor.

HELEN *(Comes in)* He's on the phone, Max. Mr.—you know. NBC. He's waiting.

MAX *(Rising)* I'll take it up in my office. (HELEN *leaves,* MAX *crosses to door)* We're not pulling down our flag. I will not break my sword over my knee for anyone. When the Roman legions, led by Augustus the Fourth, fled in defeat, he came back to win on Novembus the Fifth.

> *(He thinks about that, wonders if he got it right, nods, and leaves)*

BRIAN I think someone's got to get word to President Lincoln.

MILT Personally, I think we're one phone call away from a career in the garment center.

LUCAS *(Crossing to buffet)* Anyone mind if I take some bagels home? Just in case?

KENNY Why don't we just go back to work and write something?

VAL What have I been saying all morning?

MILT "Focking pompernickel."

> (HELEN *enters quickly)*

ACT ONE

HELEN   Listen. Ira is here. He's washing his face. He doesn't look very good to me. *(The phone rings off to their right)* Oooh, I hear my phone ringing.

(She rushes off)

KENNY *(He gets up)*   Alright, listen, everybody. Ira's going to walk in here with his Special Ailment of the day. Pneumonia, phlebitis, cataracts, whatever. No matter what he says, we pay no attention. If he faints at our feet, just let him lay there.

CAROL   That's so cruel, Kenny.

KENNY   As cruel as making us listen to his complaints every day? I don't think so.

LUCAS *(Who has been near the door)*   Here he comes.

(He rushes back to the others)

KENNY *(Softly)*   Remember. Just stare at him.

(He sits. IRA STONE enters. He is all energy with a touch of brilliant madness. He wears a topcoat and scarf)

IRA *(He holds his chest)*   I can't breathe. I can't catch my breath. I think it's a heart attack. It could be a stroke. Don't panic, just do what I tell you. *(He sits with his coat on. He talks breathlessly)* Call Columbia Presbyterian Hospital. Ask for Dr. Milton Bruckman. Tell him I got a sharp stabbing pain down my left arm, across my chest, down my back into my left leg. If he's in surgery, call Dr. Frank Banzerini at St. John's Hospital, sixth

49

floor, cardiology. Tell him I suddenly got this burning sensation in my stomach. At first I thought it was breakfast. I had smoked salmon. It was still smoking. It didn't feel right going down. If his line is busy, call the Clayton and Marcus Pharmacy on Seventy-second and Madison. Ask for Al. Tell him I need a refill on my prescription from Dr. Schneider. I can't remember the drug. Zodioprotozoc. No. Vasco something. Vasco da Dama, what the hell was it? I can't get air to my brain . . . This scarf is choking me, get it off my neck. *(He pulls it off, throws it away. No one has moved. They've all been through this before)* Don't call my wife . . . No, maybe you should call her. But don't tell her it's a stroke. If she thinks it's a stroke, she'll call my mother. I have no time to talk to my mother, she drives me crazy. *(He begins to hyperventilate and wheeze, looking to the others, who just stare)* This could be it, I swear to God. *(He still wheezes, then looks at KENNY)* Why are you just sitting there? What the hell are you waiting for?

KENNY For you to die or finish your instructions, whichever comes first.

IRA *(He gets up)* You think this is a joke? You think this is funny? You think I would walk in here with a pain so bad, I—wait a minute! *(He holds his chest)* Wait a minute! . . . Hold it! Wait a minute! *(He doesn't move)* Ohhh. *Ohhh* . . . I just passed gas! Thank God! I thought it was all over for me. *Whoo.*

MILT *(He gets up, disgusted)* Jee-sus!

CAROL *(To IRA)* I hope you die. I hope you have a stroke right now and die. I hope your mother comes and sees you and *talks to you for an hour before you die!*

IRA You're *angry?* You're upset that I'm still *alive?* What is this, Nazi Germany? Let's kill another Jew?

VAL Yes. In this case I would make an exception.

IRA Oh. Okay. Fine. Now I know who my friends are.

BRIAN Friends? What friends? You have no friends. There isn't a puppy in the world who would come out of the *pound* to live with you.

IRA *(To BRIAN)* Hey, wait a minute. From *them* I take. You haven't earned the right. Because of one goddamn Irish potato famine, I have to put up with you?

BRIAN You have the nerve to walk in here, telling us you're having a stroke and think you can fart your way out of this?

IRA *(To the others)* I had a little scare. I didn't know what it was. I'm sorry. I apologize to everyone in this room. *(To BRIAN)* Except to you. Don't blame me because someone left the Dewars White Label out of your orange juice this morning.

(BRIAN *makes a move for him,* IRA *backs away)*

KENNY Hey, come on, guys.

IRA *(He shrugs to KENNY)* It's over. Okay? . . . *(He sits)* So, read back what we got so far.

VAL What we got *so far?* You want to know what we got so far? Lucas, read him back what we got so far.

LUCAS We have nothing . . .

VAL   . . . is what we got so far.

IRA   Eleven o'clock and you've got nothing on paper? What were you people doing in here? Is it always up to *me* to get the show started?

BRIAN *(Slowly)*   You phony little faggot-looking egocentric turd. When did you ever come in on time like the rest of us?

IRA *(He laughs, amused)*   I can't believe my ears. Phony? Little faggot-looking egocentric turd?—is this what Ireland sent us? We could have had Keats. We could have had O'Casey. We could have had George Bernard Shaw. But no, we get an illiterate anti-Semite immigrant who failed streetcar conductor school. Whose father came to this country just for the free hard-boiled eggs in the saloons . . . My family, all brilliant Talmudic scholars, almost drowned coming over on the boat to America because your drunken people kept beating the shit out of the captain.

> *(*BRIAN *crosses the room. He opens the window and we hear the hum of traffic)*

CAROL   Why do we have to keep making racial jokes? Jewish jokes, Irish jokes, Italian jokes. Hasn't America *progressed* beyond that?

OTHERS *(They think for a moment)*   . . . No. Not really. I don't think so.

VAL   No. Let 'em go on. A little aggression is good for writers. All humor is based on hostility, am I right, Kenny?

KENNY   Absolutely. That's why World War II was so funny . . . Schmuck!

VAL   *(To* IRA*)*   If you didn't go to five doctors every morning, maybe you'd get here by ten o'clock.

IRA   Are you saying I'm a hypochondriac? I've had this throat problem for six months. This thing could be cancer, they don't want to tell me.

BRIAN   Have them call me and *I'll* tell you.

IRA   You goddamn leprechaun! I've been carrying you on this show for three years . . . It's in the *Encyclopaedia Britannica,* look it up. *Catholics* are not funny. Protestants are not funny. Methodists are not funny. Baptists are funny but only under water.

BRIAN   What do you want, a funny contest? You want to take on all of Christianity? Come on. Name your game.

IRA   Funny against funny?

BRIAN   For all you want.

IRA   I'll bet my shoes. My sixty-five-dollar genuine alligator Florsheims against your eight ninety-five Thom McAn cardboard funeral parlor shoes for dead men. *(He takes off his shoes and throws them into the center of the room)* There's mine. Ante up, you putz bartender.

BRIAN   You got it. *(He pulls off his shoes and tosses them next to* IRA*'s)* Okay. Pick your subject.

IRA   Funny names.

53

BRIAN   Funny names?

IRA   *(He nods)*   Funny names. Anyone else want in on this? Small bet on the side?

MILT   I'm in for a pair of shoelaces.

VAL   Alright. I give you thirty seconds to play. Then we get back to work. Alright. Are we ready?

> (BRIAN *and* IRA *take their places standing face to face, almost nose to nose, glaring at each other)*

BRIAN   *(He crosses himself)*   Up the Irish!

IRA   Out of Egypt!

VAL   Okay. For the funniest names. Ira first . . . *Go!*

IRA   Benjamin Bunjamin.

BRIAN   Angela Jonesela.

IRA   Monsignor Abe Brillstein.

BRIAN   Rabbi John Wayne.

IRA   Monica Hanukah.

BRIAN   Her Highness Queen Minnie the Moocher.

IRA   President Hi-Dee-Hi-Dee-Ho!

BRIAN   *(He shouts)*   MR. AND MRS. JESUS H. CHRIST!

IRA *(Louder)* THE EARL OF SANDWICH, HOLD THE MAYO!

BRIAN IRA STONE!

IRA *Ira Stone?* What's funny about Ira Stone?

BRIAN NOTHING! *Nothing* is funny about Ira Stone!

(BRIAN *laughs*)

IRA FOUL! DEFAULT! He broke the rules. You can't use names we know. Nobody wins.

(He picks up all four shoes, moves quickly across the room, and throws them all out the open window)

CAROL Tell me I didn't see that.

(All the others rush and look out the open window)

LUCAS *(Looking out window)* Jeez! It looks like the bombing of London.

BRIAN *(To* IRA, *furious)* Go get my shoes.

IRA They're not your shoes anymore. They belong to the people of Greater New York now.

LUCAS Direct hit on man coming out of Bergdorf Goodman's.

BRIAN *(To* IRA*)* Either you get those shoes or you better take some flying lessons real quick, you son of a bitch! You owe me two hundred dollars.

IRA Two hundred dollars for a pair of gravedigger's camping shoes?

CAROL *(Out the door)* Helen, can you come in for a second?

VAL Alright, we work all night tonight. No one leaves till we finish. And I absolutely forbid any more men's clothing to go out the window.

HELEN *(She comes in)* Yes, Carol?

CAROL Helen, would you please go downstairs and get Ira and Brian's shoes? They're on Fifty-seventh Street.

HELEN Are they being repaired?

CAROL Eventually. Ira threw them out the window.

HELEN *(To IRA)* You should have asked me, Ira. I would have taken them down.

    (HELEN exits)

KENNY *(He looks at IRA)* This man has a child who actually calls him Daddy.

IRA Oh. Oh. I see. Have I awakened the sleeping tiger? The California Whiz Kid? The reformed Jew who got Bar Mitzvahed in the Hollywood Bowl where Cantor Solomon Weiss sang the entire score to *Porgy and Bess*?

MILT *(He throws up his hands)* He's like a plague. He's like locusts. Billions of locusts. The more you kill him, the more he keeps coming back . . . In ten minutes we'll all be naked.

IRA *(To* MILT*)* I don't have a right to say what I want? When did we lose free speech?

VAL Okay, that's it. Ira, I'm asking Max to take your name off the credits this week. If you come up with something, you'll get back one letter at a time. Three jokes, you get three letters. If dot's all you come up with, it'll just say "Ira" on the screen, dot's it.

IRA Oh. Oh. Oh. Okay, what if I wrote the whole show myself? You think I can't do it? Gimme paper. *(He grabs paper off the writers' table)* Lots of paper.

(He grabs paper off the typewriter table)

BRIAN Don't forget to flush.

*(*IRA *turns back and glares at* BRIAN*)*

CAROL You really think you can do it, Ira?

IRA I think I can win the Emmy Award.

VAL I think your stroke is coming back.

KENNY Don't forget to make it funny, Ira.

IRA Funny? It says funny on my birth certificate.

KENNY Well, I didn't think it said baby.

IRA Okay. I'm going. The whole show. Top to bottom. By Ira Stone.

(He exits)

MILT   Are we on a break?—because I have to go to the john.

VAL   *There are no breaks!* We've had our breaks. We've had a bagel break, a Joe McCarthy break, a shotgun break, a hole-in-the-wall break, a Cyclantis break and a two-pairs-of-shoes-out-the-window break. We've used op all our breaks!

MILT   Well, then I'll have to ask Carol to turn around because I'm going to pee in the plant.

   (He starts to unzip his pants)

CAROL   *(She screams)*   Don't you dare!

   (She runs away from table)

LUCAS   *(To the audience)*   . . . and this was the most re-spected program in all of television . . . and I knew then and there that if I was going to keep my job, I'd have to become as totally crazy as the rest of them.

   (The second door opens, and MAX *comes in with his trench coat still on, no suit on)*

MAX   Did Helen come back with my suit yet?

CAROL   No, Max. She's out looking for shoes.

MAX   What was wrong with the shoes she was wearing?

KENNY   How'd the call go with NBC, Max?

MAX *(He sits)*   The call with NBC? *(He lights his cigar)* The call with NBC went fine.

VAL   Everything's alright?

MAX   It's fine.

CAROL   It all got settled?

MAX   It got settled fine.

BRIAN   Was anything decided?

MAX   Fine was decided. We decided fine.

VAL   No problems?

MAX   We had *some* problems but we fined them out.

VAL   That sounds fine to me, Max.

KENNY   You want to give us any details, Max? Any changes?

MAX   Changes? Let me see! . . . Oh, yes. They're cutting us back to an hour. This year is fine, next year is an hour. Next year they cut the budget. Next year they want approval of the sketches. Next year they put an observer on the show. That's all. That's the only changes. Minor stuff.

(He looks at his cigar. They can see he is controlling an explosion)

CAROL   And that's fine with you, Max?

MAX   No. That's fine with *them. Them* is fine. We is not so fine yet. But we'll see. We'll wait. We'll think. We'll plan. And then we'll be fine.

LUCAS   What is the observer going to do, Max?

MAX   The observer? He's going to observe. *(He gets up)* He'll be around the show observing the coffee, the cream cheese, the potato chips. Maybe he'll come up here and observe us working, observe Ira coming in late. *(He crosses to the telephone. He is standing behind sofa)* Maybe he'll observe me getting upset that he's observing me and then he'll observe me taking the fucking *telephone* and smashing it on the fucking floor. *(In a fury, MAX hurls the phone to the floor. He grimaces, whimpers softly, and then continues. Obviously, he has hit his foot with the phone)* Or . . . *(He steps away, limping on the foot that was hit)* if the observer is not through observing, maybe he can observe me putting my fist through his *fucking face!* (MAX *punches another hole in the wall, right next to McCarthy's hole)* And then they'll take him away for surgery and he'll observe the hospital for a while. But right now I'm fine . . . Lucas, when Helen comes back, tell her to call Tiffany's again . . . Just a simple frame with a gold plaque underneath saying, "Fine." *(He sits)* So. What have we got for this week's show?

(The door suddenly opens and IRA *comes back with the stack of paper in his hand)*

IRA   What am I crazy? *(He throws the entire stack of paper up in the air)* Write a whole show myself? Get outa here! *(He looks at* MAX*)* How you doing, Max?

MAX   Fine. Just fine.

(He calmly crosses his legs and puffs on his cigar)

Curtain

Act Two

Seven months later. Early fall. A little before ten A.M.
LUCAS *is sitting with his feet up on the writers' desk writing on a legal pad. He drinks coffee from a mug. This is a more confident, relaxed* LUCAS. *The two holes in the wall left by* MAX *are now both framed in silver. There are also two additional holes on another place on the wall. These have simple black frames, no plaques.*
LUCAS *thinks, then turns and looks at the audience.*

LUCAS *(To the audience)* It was seven months later and as you can see, I made the staff. Mug! . . . *(He holds up a coffee mug)* I was contributing a lot more to the show but what I think cemented the job for me was the day I poured lighting fluid on the desk and set fire to it . . . I was made an honorary lunatic. *(He gets up, crosses to buffet to refill his mug)* The show was cut down to an hour and the budget by a third. There were still bagels and onion rolls but no more Danish, no pound cake, no apple strudel. NBC wasn't paying anymore. Max was. *(He pours coffee)* And Max still had his temperamental moments, as you can see from the Wall of Terror . . . Those two new holes with the simple black frames were added when Ethel and Julius Rosenberg were executed . . . And although Max was valiantly trying to cut out the pills and scotch, the pressure from NBC and the sponsors made it a losing battle for him. *(The door opens and* MAX *comes in wearing a suit, no trench coat)* Oh. Hi, Max . . . This is early for you. Everything alright? *(*MAX *stands there, looks around, doesn't answer)* . . . Max?

MAX *(He looks at* LUCAS*)* What?

LUCAS How are you?

MAX No one's in yet?

LUCAS No. Just me.

MAX Just you?

LUCAS Yes, Max.

MAX So the others aren't here?

LUCAS No . . . Would you like some coffee?

MAX Usually they're in early on Tuesday.

LUCAS I know, but this is Monday, Max.

MAX *(He looks at* LUCAS*)* . . . How's your wife?

LUCAS My wife? She's fine, Max. Thanks for asking.

MAX Penny, right?

LUCAS Yes. Penny.

MAX Yeah. Pretty girl. And smart. I like her.

LUCAS Thank you, Max. I'll tell her.

MAX And the kids? How's the kids? Andy and Sue, right?

LUCAS . . . We don't have kids, Max.

MAX No kids? . . . Then who's Andy and Sue?

LUCAS   I don't know, Max.

MAX   But you like it here okay?

LUCAS   Working here? Oh, yeah. I love this job, Max.

MAX   Well, we'll see . . . So no one's here, heh?

LUCAS   No, Max. Just us.

> *(There is an awkward silence as the two stare out.* LUCAS *soon realizes that* MAX *is asleep on his feet. He starts to snore . . . then* MAX's *head falls back. As* LUCAS *takes a sip of coffee,* MAX *wakes with a start)*

MAX   Maybe I'll lie down in my office.

LUCAS   Yeah, that's a good idea.

MAX   Why?

LUCAS   Why? Well, because you look tired.

MAX   Me? Never. Never get tired. I just need a little nap, that's all.

LUCAS   I see.

MAX   So, I'll be up in my office. (MAX *starts off in the wrong direction. He catches himself and heads toward his office)* I'm gonna take a little nap.

LUCAS   Oh. Okay, Max.

> *(*MAX *starts out, stops)*

MAX   I think Andy and Sue are my nephews.

(LUCAS *nods and* MAX *leaves*)

LUCAS *(To the audience)*   That was the only time I was ever alone in a room with Max . . . It was hard finding a topic in common with him unless you were up on the Thracian Wars.

(The first door opens, and MILT *comes in wearing an all-white suit and a white Panama hat, a light blue shirt, and a tie)*

MILT   I cannot *believe* I got a ticket for speeding on the parkway. I was driving so slow, the cop who pulled me over was walking.

LUCAS   What'd you expect? You were asking for it.

MILT   *I* was?

LUCAS   You wear an all-white suit and a Panama hat, those guys sit behind a billboard waiting for some schmuck like you.

MILT   I thought I looked like a senator.

LUCAS   No. You look like a Nazi trying to catch a boat to Argentina.

MILT *(He hangs up his hat)*   I liked you better when you weren't funny.

LUCAS   Ba-dum-bum. Max was just in here.

MILT   This early? *(He looks at the wall)* No new holes.
He must be alright. What'd he say?

LUCAS   Well, he thought it was Tuesday, and he asked
me how the kids I don't have were, and then he said
he wasn't tired so he was going up to take a nap.

MILT   Well, my suit'll cheer him up. *(He looks over buffet)*
Are the bagels getting smaller or is this room getting
bigger?

LUCAS   Same size. There's just half as many now.

MILT   *(He takes a bagel)*   Well, counting my wife, that's
the second thing I lost this week.

LUCAS   Are you serious?

MILT   I'm never serious. But she always is . . . which is
why I think she's leaving.

(He cuts the bagel open)

LUCAS   I'm sorry about your wife, Milt.

MILT   *(He shrugs it off)*   Don't say anything to the guys,
will you? I want to tell Max first.

LUCAS   Yes, sure . . . You okay?

MILT   Oh, yeah. Listen, I should have known it at the
wedding. When her father handed me an empty enve-
lope, I knew it wasn't a match made in heaven.

(He pours himself some coffee)

LUCAS You don't seem too upset about it.

MILT In this room? I can't afford it. Funny is money. *(He sips coffee)* I tried to patch it up. I offered to take her on a second honeymoon. She said she didn't like the first one that much . . . Then she said, "ba-dum-bum." That's what really hurt.

LUCAS Sometimes I think you sell yourself short, Milt.

MILT Lukie, I'll sell myself in whatever size they'll buy me.

(He drinks his coffee. The door opens and VAL *enters, excited)*

VAL I just heard the news in my car. Did you hear it?

MILT No. I wasn't *in* your car.

LUCAS What happened?

*(*MILT *sits)*

VAL Stalin died. Joseph Stalin is dead.

LUCAS Really?

MILT *(To* VAL*)* So I guess you'll be going to the funeral.

VAL Milt, I want you to hear this because I've been practicing it with a tutor . . . Go *fuck* yourself!

LUCAS He said it right. *(To* VAL*)* You said it right. You actually went to a tutor to learn to say that?

VAL   Obsolutely. Cost me a focking fortune.

MILT   You mean he only taught you to say it *once?*

VAL   No. He only taught me to say it to *you* . . . So wait. There's more news. The U.S. State Department just announced they have positive proof that Russia has the hydrogen bomb.

LUCAS   Jesus! That is scary.

VAL   Tell my children. Because they're the ones who will inherit the devastation the focking politicians left them.

MILT   You know you're saying it worse than ever. You didn't go to a *Russian* tutor, did you?

VAL   This is going to be one hell of a day to write comedy. *(He looks at* MILT*)* What is that, a white suit?

MILT   Oh my God, what did the cleaners do to my blue serge?

   (He laughs at his own joke)

VAL   You didn't know Max hates white suits?

LUCAS   Max does?

VAL   Since he was a kid. No one told you about Max and white suits?

MILT   It's a joke, right? Not necessarily the kind you laugh at.

VAL I swear to God. When Max's father died, they made a mistake and buried him in someone else's white suit. Max had nightmares about it for years. Half his analysis was about white suits.

MILT I think my wife knew. She was laughing when I left the house this morning.

LUCAS Take off your jacket. Call wardrobe. Maybe they have a dark suit in your size.

MILT (*Crossing to phone*) You're telling me the truth about this, Val?

(He dials "one")

VAL If Max sees you in that suit, Tiffany's does some business today.

MILT (*Into the phone*) Helen, could you get me wardrobe, please . . . No, *now*. I need an emergency dark suit. I'll hold.

(The door opens)

LUCAS Hi, Momma.

(CAROL *enters. She is very, very pregnant, about the end of her eighth month. She walks with great caution*)

CAROL Please! Nobody stand between me and that chair.

LUCAS You need any help?

CAROL   No, thanks. I've had enough help from men. *(She sees* MILT *and screams)* Oh, God! I thought you were a doctor. I was afraid I miscounted my due date.

LUCAS *(Helping her toward her chair)*   When *is* your due date?

CAROL   Whenever my doctor's out of town.

MILT *(Into the phone)*   Come on. Come on. Come on.

CAROL   I'm moving as fast as I can.

LUCAS *(Still helping her)*   You want to put your feet up?

CAROL   Another gynecologist?

    (She sits)

VAL   Did you hear about Joseph Stalin?

CAROL   Don't tell me. McCarthy put him on the blacklist.

MILT *(Into the phone)*   Hello, wardrobe? Who's this? . . . Hannah? . . . Listen, Hannah. This is Milt Fields, one of the writers. We're working on a sketch here and we need a dark suit, size forty regular. As soon as possible . . . Yes. Yes, that sounds fine . . . No, I can't come downtown. We need it here in the writers' room . . . Would you, please? Take a taxi. God bless you, Hannah. I love you. *(He hangs up, then quickly dials "one." Aside to* VAL) Be right with you. *(Into the phone)* Helen? Milt . . . Max is up in his office. I want you to call me in here the *second* he comes down. The exact minute you see his feet, you call me immediately. Someone's life, who we both love very much, depends on this. Okay? *(He hangs up. He gets up, then says to* LUCAS*)* Lucas, when she calls me, I'll rush into the men's room. I'll stay there until Hannah gets here, then you bring the suit to me in the john.

(BRIAN *walks in in his drab suit with ash marks on it)*

BRIAN So the Ruskees got the Big Bazoom. Joe McCarthy is suddenly very popular in America today. *(*BRIAN *laughs, crosses to the food counter)* Great suit, Milt. You look like the governor of Devil's Island.

MILT Oh. Mr. Fashion Plate. The man's been wearing a single-breasted ash tray for three years.

BRIAN *(He wipes ashes off his lapel)* That's right. And I'll be wearing it opening night of my new play. Why don't you wait outside the theater and watch the crowds mob me?

MILT Oh. His new "play." *A Streetcar named Failure.*

(KENNY *walks in, distressed)*

KENNY Where's Max?

LUCAS Up in his office.

KENNY We have to talk. We got a problem.

CAROL *(She holds her stomach)* As bad as being kicked in the stomach?

MILT *(To* KENNY*)*   No joke about my suit? You're going to deprive me of your wit? You're not going to tell me what I look like?

KENNY   The first rabbi in the Amazon. Come on. This is serious business. I heard from Max again, he got a call yesterday from Aaron, his business manager. *(*CAROL *starts to sob softly)* The show's been over budget every week this season. According to Max's deal . . . Is somebody crying?

CAROL   It's me. I'm sorry, I need a release.

> *(She sobs softly. They all look at her, like they're watching a bus accident)*

KENNY *(To* CAROL*)*   . . . Is this going to take long? We got business here.

CAROL *(Annoyed)*   Oh. I'm sorry. Is it *annoying* you?

MILT   No! . . . But if you could do it later . . .

KENNY   Leave her alone . . . This is important. Max called me three times last night. Every time he tried to tell me what it was, he broke down. He got a call yesterday from Aaron, his business manager. The show's been over budget every week this season. According to Max's deal, Max is responsible for the overage. He owes the network about a third of his salary so far.

CAROL   Wait a minute! *Wait a minute!! (She feels her stomach)* . . . The baby's moving!

MILT   ARE YOU GIVING BIRTH?

CAROL   God, I hope not. It's moving up. Towards my head.

MILT   Where the hell is it going?

CAROL   I think it just wants to look out of my eyes.

KENNY   Listen to me, will you? . . . You know Max. He wants the best costumes, the best sets, the best of everything. Only now it's costing him big. So Aaron laid down the law. Cut down on costumes, on sets, on everything.

VAL   I obsolutely agree. There's too much waste around here.

KENNY   Now this comes from Aaron, not Max. He's cutting one person from costumes, one from sets, one from the camera crew, one from the secretaries—and this is where Max broke down in tears—one from the writing staff.

   (*There is a numb silence as everyone leans back*)

MILT   I cannot *fucking believe* I wore a white suit today.

   (*He sinks in his chair*)

KENNY   Somebody has to go, guys. Max is not going to pick him. Aaron is. Aaron, who was once Heinrich Himmler's accountant, is not an easy man to deal with . . . So that's it. One of us is going.

VAL   This is a very bad dilemma.

MILT   Why, you've heard of a good dilemma?

CAROL Look, in a couple of weeks I'm leaving to have my baby. I'll be out about two months. That buys us some time, doesn't it?

KENNY Aaron's not looking to buy time. He's looking to get rid of one salary for the entire year.

VAL But we have contracts, no?

KENNY No. We have three-month options. In case NBC canceled. Didn't your agent tell you?

VAL He plays golf a lot. I don't like to bother him.

LUCAS Who are we kidding? I'm the logical choice. I'm the last one on the staff. You all have seniority. So I go.

VAL Over my dead body. Obsolutely not. Out of the question. No one has to volunteer for this.

LUCAS I'm not volunteering. I'm just saying they'll probably pick me because I'm the most expendable.

VAL Oh. Well, if that's the case, that's different.

KENNY The irony is Lucas is the safest one here. He makes a third of what most of the staff makes. What Aaron wants is to get rid of one of the top money guys.

BRIAN Well, I guess I have to be the one to say this. Who's the one on this show who makes *top* money and puts in half the time of anyone else? Pay him by the hour and Max would save almost an entire salary. I'm not naming any names.

KENNY So Ira goes? Anyone second the betrayal?

VAL   Obsolutely not. We're starting our own blacklist here.

KENNY   Hey, guys. We don't make the choice who goes. Aaron does. And that's it unless someone comes up with an unforeseen miracle.

(*The door opens and* IRA *rushes in with a pained expression*)

IRA   They think I have a brain tumor.

KENNY *(To the others)*   This may be what we're looking for.

CAROL *(To* IRA*)*   Who thinks you have a brain tumor?

IRA   I couldn't tie my shoelaces this morning. I forgot how to do it. *Shoelaces!* . . . My three-year-old kid tied his, I *begged* him to do mine. I poured tomato juice into my coffee. Tomato juice.

BRIAN   Well, it isn't necessarily a brain tumor. Have you ruled out stupidity?

IRA   Remember to say that at my funeral. After you do your little jig on my coffin.

CAROL   Ira, calm down.

IRA   This *is* calm down. This is the best I've been all day.

BRIAN   Listen, there could be a lot of reasons for this, Ira. Maybe you're just underworked.

IRA *(to* BRIAN*)*   You can't wait, can you? You're dying to come to the hospital and sing "Oh, Danny Boy" at my bedside.

CAROL *(To* BRIAN*)*   Leave him alone, Brian. If he wants a brain tumor, let him have a brain tumor.

IRA *(He puts his hand over his eyes)*   I have double vision.

LUCAS   You mean right now?

IRA   Right now, all night, all morning. Double vision. Two cabs pulled up in front of my house this morning. I took them both.

VAL   Ira! Since I know you, you've had every disease known to mankind and a few animal diseases. And you're still here.

CAROL   You don't have a brain tumor.

IRA *(He shouts)*   You want proof? Undeniable, positive, absolute proof? *(He crosses to desk, picks up a thick pointed black pen, and prints in large bold letters,* I HAVE A BRAIN TUMOR*)* There! There it is in black and white! Okay?

CAROL   You actually wrote on the wall with an indelible marker? A mother would drown her child for doing that.

> *(*IRA *sits, looks at* MILT*)*

IRA   I'm seeing double again . . . Milt, will you sit down, please? You look like the entrance to the White House.

KENNY Ira, we're busy. If you got a brain tumor go down to the shoemaker, he'll take it out.

IRA Oh, I see. I'm crazy, right? Like Tolstoy was crazy. Like Dostoevsky was crazy.

KENNY No. They were crazy in a talented way. You're sort of a fucking waste of time crazy.

VAL *(To* IRA*)* Either you stay in this room and you write with us together or you go home and have your kid untie your laces and come in tomorrow.

IRA Did I say no? I'm here. I came to work, didn't I? *(He crosses to desk on other side of room)* I just have to see how my stocks are doing.

CAROL *(To* IRA*)* Has it ever occurred to you that you monopolize every minute you're in this room?

IRA Who better than me? What am I, uninteresting?

(HELEN *rushes into the room)*

HELEN Milt! Max is coming in.

MILT *Now?* I told you to call me!

(MAX *walks into the room.* MILT *gets down on all fours and hides between* CAROL *and the coffee table.* MAX *seems very energized)*

MAX *(To* HELEN*)* No calls for anyone. Nobody leaves, nobody moves. We have to talk in here.

(He hangs up his suit jacket)

HELEN   Yes, Max . . . Sorry, Milt.

(She goes, MILT *lets out a groan.* MAX *looks at* CAROL, *who imitates* MILT'*s groan)*

MAX *(He squints over toward* MILT*)*   Who's that? Milt? What's the matter with you?

MILT *(He starts to get up)*   Don't feel too good. I'll be right back. Have to go to the john.

(He gets up, grabbing a newspaper, and shields his body with it, then walks quickly toward the door)

MAX   Save it. We got to talk first. Siddown.

MILT   Two minutes, Max. I'll rush.

MAX *(He looks at* MILT*)*   Are you sick? You look white as a ghost.

MILT   I get that way. I think it's a bladder infection.

MAX   No. Something else. Something different. Why do you look different?

MILT *(He's lost)*   I—I don't know, Max.

(He tries covering himself with the newspaper in an effort to hide some of the white)

MAX *(Suddenly pointing at him)*   Ahh!

MILT *(He recoils in terror)*   Ahh!

MAX   *Ahh!*

79

MILT *Ahh!*

MAX . . . You got a haircut, right?

MILT Me? Yes. This morning. Just a light trim. Amazing you noticed.

MAX A man gets a haircut, I notice. Siddown. (MILT *goes to the waste basket by the bagel table and sits down on the opposite side of the room. With hand to his mouth,* MAX *calls*) Not over there. I'm not talking over there.

MILT I want to be near the water so I can drink. I can hear you.

(MILT *is sitting on the wastebasket*)

MAX *(He shields his eyes)* Don't sit in the sun. There's a glare on you. *(He turns)* Okay. Where's Carol?

CAROL Here, Max.

MAX Anything new with the baby?

CAROL No. Nothing new. Still in there.

MAX You got a good doctor?

CAROL Oh, yeah. Very good. I love my doctor.

MAX You're in love with your doctor?

CAROL No. I love that he's a good doctor. I love my husband.

MAX   That's right. You're still with your husband. Good.
I'm glad . . . (VAL *is right behind him*) Where's Val?

VAL *(He's never moved)*   Right here, Max.

MAX *(He yells)   You keep moving around! Sit on one place!*

VAL   Absolutely. Forgive me. My fault.

   (He sits at the writers' table)

MAX   So, Kenny . . . did you . . .

   (MAX *whispers in* KENNY's *ear*)

KENNY   What?

MAX   . . . Did you . . .

   (MAX *whispers again in* KENNY's *ear*)

KENNY   What?

MAX *(He yells)*   DID YOU TELL THEM ABOUT
OUR PHONE CALL?

KENNY   Yes, Max. I told everyone when I came in.

CAROL   We heard, Max.

MAX   I hope it didn't upset the baby.

CAROL   I don't think so. She's not into show business yet.

MAX   Our children are all we have. They can take everything else away from you. Your dignity, your pride,

your set designers, your makeup lady, but they can't take your children. You understand what I'm saying?

CAROL   Yes, Max.

MAX   So far no one's going. So far everyone's still here.

VAL   That's good, Max.

MAX   But so far is only going to last so far. Then so far turns into so long.

KENNY   We understand, Max.

IRA   Understand what? What are you talking about?

MAX   He doesn't know?

KENNY   Ira came in late.

MAX *(To* IRA*)*   What'd I tell everybody about coming in late?

IRA   What do I know? I'm never here when you tell them.

(MAX *begins to walk toward* IRA *when suddenly* MAX*'s eyes go to the wall. He squints as he looks at it, then turns to the others)*

MAX   "I Have a Brain Tumor"? . . . Who wrote that?

IRA   I did.

MAX   Don't lie to me. Who wrote it?

IRA   I just told you. It was me.

MAX   Did someone from NBC do this? Is that what they're trying to tell me? I have a brain tumor? So they can break the contract?

IRA   Max, I swear to God. On my father's grave. On my children's life. I wrote it.

MAX   Why?

IRA   Because I have a brain tumor.

MAX   Is that going to wash off?

IRA   Don't you care what may happen to me?

MAX   First let's take care of what happened to my wall . . . Is that going to wash off?

IRA   No. It's not. It's a permanent marker, okay?

MAX   If this doesn't wash off, you'll definitely have a brain tumor. *(He crosses back to his chair, then sits)* Alright, Kenny. Tell him about our phone call.

KENNY   *(To* IRA*)* You know all about the budget problems the show's been having this year . . . Well, Max has been paying a lot of things out of his own pocket . . .

IRA   Wait a minute! Wait a minute! *(To* MAX*)* Look at the holes you punched in there. It's a polka-dot wall. And I get blamed for a few lousy words scribbled in ink?

MAX *(He gets up)* It's my wall. It's my holes. You wanna buy your own wall, this one's for sale. *(He points to the wall IRA wrote on)* Take it. For five thousand dollars you can cover it with your entire life's blood pressure . . . Otherwise I want my wall back the way it was. Go on, Kenny.

> *(He sits again)*

KENNY *(To IRA)* This is the last time I'm telling you. Aaron won't let Max pay for anything anymore. You hear what I'm telling you? So they're cutting one person from every department on the show? You listening? . . . Which means one writer, one of us, someone in this room, has to go. That's it.

IRA What are you saying? That one of you guys has to go?

KENNY I say we hang him out the window. Make him a permanent weather vane.

IRA Oh, you mean it includes *everybody* . . . Oh, this is funny. This is *The Human Comedy*. This is William Saroyan. This is Reality. I would have come early for this. *(He sits)* Okay, so how does it work? How do we pick the one who goes?

MILT *(Is on the other side of the room. He stands)* We don't. Aaron is going to pick him.

MAX *(Stands, looks at him suspiciously)* What color is that suit?

> *(MILT backs away nervously)*

MILT   This? This is an off-color cream-beige, sort of a taupe antique eggshell.

MAX   *(He looks at him)*   You're sure that's not a . . . ?

MILT   No, no, no, no, it isn't.

MAX   Alright. Upstairs I thought it out. There's another way. A better way. We don't need Aaron to pick someone.

(He sits)

BRIAN   This sounds hopeful, Max. How do we do it?

(MAX motions for them to lean in. They all lean in)

MAX   . . . Is Napoleon dead?

VAL   What do you mean?

MAX   I asked a simple question. Is Napoleon dead?

VAL   Yes, Max. He is. Napoleon is dead.

MAX   How do you know? Did you see him dead?

VAL   Not personally, no. But I saw his tomb in Paris.

MAX   Did you open the tomb and look?

VAL   They don't let you do that, Max. And who could lift it? It was just me and my wife.

MAX   So how do you know he's in the tomb?

VAL It says so. Why would they build Napoleon's tomb if he wasn't in it?

MAX They built the Eiffel Tower, they didn't put Mr. Eiffel in it.

KENNY Mr. Kellogg isn't in his box of corn flakes either, Max. What point are you trying to make?

MAX I just made it. Maybe we can fire a writer, but no one has to go.

BRIAN How do we do that, Max?

MAX Easy. I worked it all out. I cut all your salaries down ten percent. Then I fire a writer. Doesn't make any difference who. Then I take all the ten percents and I pay the fired writer. So he stays. And then I pay your ten percents back out of miscellaneous expenses. So the IRS gets paid, all the writers get paid, no one gets fired and it doesn't cost me anything.

KENNY And when they ask where the miscellaneous expenses are, what do you say?

MAX *They're in Napoleon's tomb!* WHAT DO I KNOW? I DON'T WANT TO HEAR ANY MORE. I thought it all out, it works for me. Let Aaron figure out the details. I don't want to fire anyone. My writers are my flesh and blood. There is no miscellaneous in my body, you understand? Now get Helen in here, we got a show to write.

VAL Lucas, get Helen in here.

MILT *I'll do it!*

86

(He prances by on tiptoes, then rushes out of the room)

MAX *(He looks at him go)* . . . I think he hangs out with ballet dancers.

LUCAS *(To the audience)* So we finally went to work. We usually based our sketches on what was currently in the news.

> *(HELEN comes in quickly, crosses behind MAX and hands out paper to all the writers)*

The movie version of *Julius Caesar* starring Marlon Brando just opened on Broadway. *(They all get their scripts)* . . . so we worked on it all morning and all afternoon.

MAX *(To HELEN)* Okay! Read back what we got.

HELEN From the top?

MAX From the top.

HELEN *(She reads)* Titles . . . High Class Films Presents . . . William Shakespeare's *Julius Caesar* . . . Produced by Nigel Bagel . . . Screenplay by Peter Porter and Esther Lester . . . Directed by Sir John Malcolm and his wife, Gloria . . . and starring James Hedgehog, Morris Porridge, Olivia Malaria, and Marlon Merlin, in his first completely memorized part, as Julius Caesar . . . Rome, forty-four B.C. . . . Outside the Roman Senate . . .

IRA Not outside the Roman Senate. Two blocks from the Roman Senate. Two *blocks* is funny.

> *(HELEN looks at MAX, who nods approval)*

87

HELEN *(She writes, then reads again)* Two blocks from the Roman Senate . . . Brutus speaks.

KENNY *(Reading)* Hail, Cassius.

BRIAN Hail, Brutus.

KENNY What news from Flavius and Lepidus?

BRIAN Not well. Flavius has mucus and Lepidus is nauseous.

KENNY *(Reading)* Hark! Trebonius approaches . . . Hail, Trebonius. How fare thee?

VAL *(Reading)* A slight pain in my kishkas.

CAROL You think they'll know what kishkas are in Nebraska, Max?

MAX If you point to it and make a face, they'll know . . . Go on.

BRIAN What news of the conspiracy?

VAL Linus told Paulus. Paulus thinks it's much hocus-pocus. Yet Flavius and Lepidus told Marcus that justice must be practiced.

MAX Okay, hold it! Enough with the shmokus pokus dokus. You'll milk it to death. Cut the Linus Paulus Pokus . . . Go on.

BRIAN And of the conspiracy. What of it does Caesar know?

VAL   Caesar knows not of that which has yet to become knownst. For if knownst, he becomes of our conspired thoughts, then would Caesar not give value to constrain such concerns?

KENNY   Of that I know not, but that which I do know concerns all conspirators, thus giving recourse to Caesar's compliance to which he has not yet given his dispensation.

BRIAN   Then it dost fall upon our devoted intentions, that Caesar must not become martyred, for all Rome would give spleen to those that hasten his death which seeks out the profit of this foul and festered—

MAX   *(He stands on a chair behind them, then yells)*   ALRIGHT! ENOUGH! Get me into the goddamn sketch already. Maybe last year when we had an hour and a half, we could do "what gives spleen to Linus and Paulus upon his martyred kishkas," but this is *this* year, for crise sakes.

HELEN   *(Looking at the script)*   I don't have that line here, Max.

CAROL   *(To* HELEN*)*   Try to pay attention, sweetheart.

(The door opens and MILT *comes in. He tries to be inconspicuous. He is now wearing a dark suit with the cuffs and the pants much too short. He still has on the white shoes and white socks)*

MILT   *(Softly)*   Sorry. Just had to go to the john.

(He crosses to the sofa with CAROL *and looks at pages of the sketch.* MAX *looks at him in disbelief)*

MAX   What'd you do, shave? You look different again.

MILT   No. Just washed up.

MAX   I hate your suit. You wear weird things, you know that? *(MILT nods. MAX looks at KENNY, VAL, and BRIAN, who nod consent. MAX turns to HELEN)* Okay. Go on.

HELEN   It's Cassius' line.

BRIAN   Caution. Caesar is upon us . . . Hail, Caesar.

KENNY and VAL   Hail, oh mighty Caesar.

HELEN   Max looks up into the sky. They all look up too.

KENNY   What dost thou seekest in the constellations, Caesar?

MAX   *(Reads, doing Brando)*   A clustuh a stahs in da heavens.

BRIAN   And by what name dost this cluster be called, oh, Caesar?

MAX   It is called Stelluh . . . *Stelluh!* . . . Stelluh for Stahlight! *(MAX smiles as MAX)* That's good. I like that . . . Good joke, Kenny.

IRA   *(Jumps up)*   Kenny? What do you mean, Kenny? That's my joke.

MAX   Who cares?

IRA   I care. I like to be given credit for what I contribute. That's my joke, Max.

KENNY He's right, Max! It was his.

MAX It makes no difference . . . I don't want no prima madonnas in here.

IRA *(He laughs)* Prima *madonnas?* . . . You know why you're funny, Max? Because you're the only one who doesn't understand what you're saying.

MAX Really? How about this? . . . You're fired, Ira . . . I understood *that*. *That* made sense to me. I thought that was *extremely* clear.

IRA *(He laughs)* I'm fired?

MAX Yes. You're prima unemployed.

IRA Max, I know I'm a little nuts. But on the line of crazies, you're a mile and a half ahead of me.

MAX Oh, I see. You're sane and I'm crazy.

IRA Don't take my word for it. Ask my shrink. We've been analyzing you for the last ten months.

MAX You had *me* analyzed?

IRA Right. We finished me last year, so this year we did you. He thinks you're a comic genius. He worships you, Max. Nobody makes him laugh the way you do. But he thinks you're capable of going to the Bronx Zoo and killing all the gorillas.

MAX I'll tell you what. I fire you and I fire him. He can't analyze me anymore. And if I see him, he'll be the first gorilla.

IRA   I'm fired.

MAX   Yes.

IRA   Fine. Great . . . I want my Stelluh joke back.

MAX   NO STELLUH! I paid for Stelluh. I own Stelluh. You can have Linus Paulus Hokus Dokus, you can have "he knows not what he naught knoweth who Pepidus is," but Stelluh is mine!

IRA   I give you Stelluh on one condition.

MAX   No, sir. No conditions.

VAL   Max, hear his condition. What's your condition, Ira?

IRA   You used to tell me, but you never say it anymore, Max. I just want you to say you love me.

MAX   *(He gets up, fire in his eyes)*   *Love* him? . . . Love *that*? . . . He steals my Stelluh and he wants my *love*? (To IRA) You dreckus schmuckus pyuckiss, toochis!

KENNY   You want to think it over a few minutes, Max?

MAX   *(Jumps on IRA)*   I want my salary back. Four years' salary. *(The guys pull MAX off)* And I want my holding tax and my social security and the toy trucks I sent your kid.

IRA   *(He walks over to HELEN)*   Excuse me, sweetheart. *(He takes a page out of her hand, tears out a small piece of the page, then gives her the page back)* Okay. I took

Stelluh. If anyone tries to put it in the show, I will make a group citizen's arrest. I can outcrazy you any-time, Max.

MAX *(He blocks* IRA*'s way)*   Paste it back on the page or I'll staple you and your brain tumor to the wall.

IRA   I'm leaving now. And Stelluh's going with me.

MAX *(He holds out his hand)*   Give it to me, Ira. Give it to me. Because I'm starting to get one of my Wolf Man headaches.

IRA   You fired me. I gave you your chance. You won't tell me you love me, fine. Say goodbye to Stelluh. *(He puts it in his mouth and chews it.* MAX *steams)* I'll tell you something. It's a funny joke but it tastes like shit.

> *(There is a tense moment as* MAX *just stares at* IRA. *Slowly at first,* MAX *begins to laugh. One by one the guys join him until finally everyone is laughing.* MAX *puts his arm around* IRA *in a friendly fashion, then flings* IRA *down on the table. The others try vainly to pull* MAX *off)*

MAX   If you swallow it, I shove my arm down your throat, and pull Stelluh out with your tonsils.

CAROL   Max, it's just a piece of paper. We can write it again.

IRA *(Gasping)*   Not until he says he loves me.

MILT   Somebody get a torch. Maybe fire will frighten them.

IRA *(To* MAX*)*   I love *you,* you schmuck. Why don't you love me?

MAX   I *like* you, but I love Stelluh. Spit it out.

IRA   No. You gotta say it. Make him say it, somebody.

MILT *(To* CAROL*)*   Sort of like a Eugene O'Neill play, isn't it?

IRA *(Gasping)*   Alright, alright. *(He spits, and the wad of paper sails across the room)* Jesus! I'm glad I didn't write *War and Peace.*

MAX *(To* HELEN*)*   Put it back in the script.

HELEN *(She points to wet paper on the floor)*   You mean *that*?

CAROL   No. Just type it back in again. The Smithsonian will pick that up later.

MAX   Okay. I got what I wanted. Now I love you, you bastard.

IRA   Am I still fired?

MAX   No. Val is fired.

VAL   Why me?

MAX   Just for an hour. Everyone has to take his turn.

BRIAN   What about you?

MAX   Absolutely. I'm fired after Lucas. Everyone except Carol. I'm not firing a pregnant woman.

CAROL   Really? Since when did anyone here ever notice I was a woman?

MILT   I knew the first day when you took your coat off. It took me a couple of hours, but I noticed.

CAROL   Well, I don't want to be considered a woman. I want to be considered a writer.

BRIAN   Fine with me, you'll just have to shave like the rest of us.

MAX   What are we talking about here? *(To* CAROL*)* What's wrong with being a woman? My wife's a woman, she's crazy about it.

CAROL   I like it too, Max, but not in here. I can't survive in here as a woman. But as a writer, I can hold my own with anyone.

MAX   I'm sorry. You *have* to be a woman. The show needs a woman's point of view. Of everybody here, you come the closest.

CAROL   After five years in here, Max, you think I know what a woman's point of view is? I come home at night smelling from cigar smoke, I have to put my dress in a humidor . . . I never said a crude word in my life before I came here. But now I go home to my fucking house and talk to my fucking husband like a fucking sailor . . . It's okay. I don't mind. If you lived in France for five years, you'd speak French. But I'm not *in*

France. I'm here so I speak fuck . . . I don't want to be called a woman writer. I want to be called a *good* writer, and if it means being one of the guys then I'll be one of the guys. I can handle it.

MILT *(To* CAROL*)*   Well, I agree. And I hope you have a great baby there, fella.

MAX   Okay. Back to work. Where were we?

HELEN   Caesar has the next line.

MAX *(As Brando)*   Whad is wrong? Whad is dis feeling of doom dat hangs in duh night air? What is dis twelve-inch kitchen knife doing in my back? Oh boy. Dis hoits.

KENNY   Oh, foul deed. Dost thou forgive me, Caesar?

MAX   Oh, Brudus, Brudus, my brudder . . . I depended on thee . . . I counted on thee . . . I coulda been a contender . . .

CAROL   Caesar.

MAX   It's time.

CAROL   Caesar.

MAX   I have a date with death. Wait in the chariot, honey. I'll be right with you.

HELEN   They plunge another dagger in him.

> (MAX *does a series of death throes, then falls on his face)*

MAX TAXI!

KENNY The deed is done. Caesar reigns no more.

MAX *(He raises his head)* It stopped raining?

    (He falls back again)

BRIAN We pray for your soul, Caesar.

BRIAN, KENNY, and VAL Adonday donis latinum moray quantis bellum Nostre Damus losto.

MAX Nostre Damus lost? Against Southern Californus?

HELEN That's where we stopped writing, Max.

MAX I need a finish. Something to end my speech. Something big.

IRA I got it, Max. *(He lies down flat on the floor on his stomach)* You pull yourself up from the ground. *(He starts to pull himself up)* . . . then you get on one knee . . . *(He gets on one knee)* and you spread your arms out to Rome. *(He spreads his arms out)* And then you sing . . . *(To the tune of "Swanee")*

    Roma, how I love ya, how I love ya,
    My dear old Roma
    I'd give the world to be
    Among the folks in "Fatza goona poppalini"
    Roma, how I love ya, how I love ya
    My dear old Roma
    The folks at home will see me no more
    Till I get to that pasta shore . . .

MAX "Fatza goona poppalini"? . . . The man is crazy
. . . but I like it. Put it in the sketch.

*(They join in singing and leave the stage as the lights
come down)*

LUCAS *(To the audience)* We wrote that week's show and
the next week's show and the next two months' shows
. . . *(LUCAS is alone. He stands in a light over at the side
of the stage. The others have all left)* The quality was still
there but the ratings weren't. America wanted comedy
closer to their own lives. Julius Caesar wasn't as famil-
iar to them as kids named Beaver and fathers who knew
best. Max never really had to fire anyone because Brian
soon left for Hollywood. There was a definite air of
gloom around the office because Max was becoming
more and more disoriented. He was in constant
negotiations with NBC about the future of the show
and they took a hard line. It didn't stop Max from
throwing his annual festive Christmas party, but he did,
however, punch a large hole in the elevator door
. . . Now you didn't have to look up to see what floor
you were on . . . *(We hear Christmas music coming up
softly from the outer offices and we see a lit Christmas tree
in the corner of the room . . . A light snowfall can be seen
through the windows)* . . . To be honest, we were all a
little frightened. Because until now, we all had each
other to lean on. But like little chicks leaving the nest,
we'd soon know the fear, the panic, and the courage
needed to fly by ourselves.

(The light goes out on LUCAS.
The lights come back on in the office. It is night.
LUCAS is gone. The Christmas music is a little louder,
and we can hear the chatter from the outside office.

MILT *walks in in a neat double-breasted suit. He carries a glass and a half-empty bottle of champagne)*

MILT . . . So I get the petition for divorce in the mail yesterday, you hear? . . . Two days before Christmas . . . We worked out a nice settlement though. She gave me a beautiful picture of the house . . . *(He turns around)* Where are you? . . . Helen? *(He looks out in the hall)* Come on in. It's too noisy out there.

(HELEN *comes in cautiously. She is wearing a simple black dress, cut revealingly in the front, her hair up. We see for the first time what a handsome woman* HELEN *is. She has a glass of champagne in hand)*

HELEN I don't mind the noise. It's a party, isn't it?

MILT My goodness, Helen, that dress is so becoming to you. Listen, Helen. I'm going to say something now that may shock you. But just hear me out. Because I say it with all sincerity and with my deepest regard and respect for you . . . You're very attracted to me, aren't you?

HELEN Actually, I'm not.

MILT But a little, right?

HELEN No. Not even a little.

MILT You didn't tell Giselle in the office that you thought I was cute?

HELEN *Me?* No. Never. Why would I say that? *Cute?* Oh, God, no.

MILT   Maybe it was Giselle who said I was cute.

HELEN   No. Giselle told me she thought *Kenny* was cute.

MILT   Alright. So what are we talking about? Semantics.

HELEN   I think I should be getting back.

MILT   What if I said that I wasn't interested in an affair? What if I said what I really wanted is a deep and lasting relationship?

HELEN   I hope you find it. I really do.

MILT   What if I offered to give you my next year's salary for one night? . . . No, don't believe that. There may not be a show next year.

HELEN   I know.

MILT   I'd be out of a job, out of a wife, out of a family . . . Does pity excite you in any way?

HELEN   I really don't want to miss the party . . .

MILT   What kind of a guy *are* you looking for?

HELEN   I'm not looking for anyone.

MILT   Then what is it you want?

HELEN   I want to be a writer. I want to write comedy.

MILT   A *comedy* writer? . . . Oi vey! . . . Why? You really want to be like me? Like Val? Like Ira? Like any of us?

HELEN   More than anything else in the world.

MILT   Helen! You *know* us. We're disgusting. We're children. We have no life. This room is our life. We curse each other, hate each other. We throw shoes out the window, we set fire to the desk. We've made obscene phone calls to St. Patrick's Cathedral. We'll humiliate and denigrate anyone or anything in the world just to get a laugh.

HELEN   See, that excites me.

MILT   I'll teach you everything I know.

> *(He takes her hand and begins to rub it. VAL walks in wearing his best suit. He holds a glass of vodka. He is drunk)*

VAL   Max wants all the writers in here. He wants to make a toast.

MILT   First the Danish goes, then the bagels. Now we're down to toast.

HELEN   No, I think he means with champagne.

MILT *(To HELEN)*   Maybe you should rethink this comedy thing.

> *(LUCAS enters, wearing a suit, carrying a bottle of beer)*

LUCAS   Did you guys hear what McCarthy did? Practically on Christmas Eve?

VAL He put the Pope on the blacklist. Now the Pope can't get work on TV or in the movies. *(He laughs)* Can you imagine how drunk I must be to say that?

> (BRIAN *walks in wearing a sprightly houndstooth sports jacket, a hat, tan slacks, loafers, and a cashmere coat, with the ever-present cigarette in his mouth)*

BRIAN Who's got a camera? I want you to see what success looks like.

LUCAS *(He shakes* BRIAN*'s hand)* I knew you were in town. I heard you coughing.

MILT Brianchkila! I thought you were going to send for me.

BRIAN I didn't know you delivered.

MILT *(To* HELEN*)* See. One day you'll say funny things like that.

LUCAS Jeez, you really went Hollywood. I bet that coat has a little swimming pool in the pocket.

BRIAN *(He snaps his fingers)* I sold out like that. I am now not only richer than you guys, I'm also three hours younger.

HELEN Ba-dum-bum-ba-dum-bum-bum-ba-dum.

MILT *(To* HELEN*)* Later we'll have a little talk about timing.

VAL *(He squints)* Who's that? Is that Brian? Where the hell were you?

BRIAN You just noticed I've been gone for three months?

VAL Hey, Brian. Have you heard the news?

BRIAN What?

VAL I'm so pissed, I don't give a shit.

MILT *(To* HELEN*)* Russian humor. It's funnier if you're on a mule.

LUCAS *(To* BRIAN*)* So where you living out there?

BRIAN Oh, a little place in the hills overlooking Yvonne DeCarlo.

HELEN God, I'd give *anything* to live in Hollywood.

MILT Well, that's all it takes, honey.

> (CAROL *walks in in a smart suit. Her old slim figure is back again)*

CAROL Brian! I heard you were in here. Come here. I haven't hugged a Gentile in so long. *(They hug. She feels his coat)* Oh, my God. Is that cashmere?

BRIAN One hundred per cent. (BRIAN *removes his hat; He has a full head of hair)* My hair is coming in that way too . . . You look terrific, Momma. I heard you had a boy.

CAROL No. A girl.

BRIAN Well, don't worry. He'll grow out of it.

(KENNY *walks in*)

KENNY   Will someone take my turn with Max while he's throwing up? I pulled his head out of the john so much, I feel like a lifeguard . . . Brian! How are you? (BRIAN *starts to answer but coughs and coughs*) I never heard a pack of Camels talk before.

CAROL   Max looks terrible. What's he been drinking, Kenny?

KENNY   Piña colonics, I don't know . . . The man just ate a roast beef sandwich the size of a Buick.

CAROL   Couldn't you stop him?

KENNY   With what? A harpoon?

(*They laugh*)

MILT   Keep going, Kenny. You're on a roll.

KENNY   If I was on a roll, Max would eat me too. (*They all laugh*)

BRIAN (*He looks at his watch*)   Listen, I just wanted to say hello. My kids are downstairs. I'm taking them to Mass.

MILT   Mass? Isn't that in Boston?

HELEN   No. They have them in New York too.

MILT (*To* HELEN)   Maybe you should write children's stories.

(IRA *bursts into the room in galoshes and a topcoat over a blue suit*)

IRA   I was just on my way to St. John's Hospital. I felt a funny feeling in my back, like a broken spine or something . . . So wait'll you hear this . . . About a Chinese Jew.

BRIAN   Okay. He's setting us up. A Chinese Jew. Don't tell us his name. Give us one crack at it . . . Seymour Dragon.

MILT   Solomon Take-Out.

KENNY   Charley Chanstein.

CAROL   Pincus Ping Pong.

BRIAN   Pincus Ping Pong is good . . .

HELEN   Can I say one?

(*They all look at her*)

MILT   I don't know if we're all drunk enough to hear this.

BRIAN (*To* HELEN)   You understand the rules? He has to have a Chinese-Jewish name.

HELEN   I know. I get it.

MILT   Listen, who knows? . . . Go ahead, sweetheart. Kill 'em.

HELEN *(She thinks . . . a long time)* Let's see . . . er . . . er . . . *(The others sit down)* Sidney . . . Sidney . . . Can I take back Sidney?

KENNY Good move, kid.

HELEN Oh. Oh. I got it . . . Stephen . . . Stephen . . .

CAROL Helen, can I ask you something? Is Stephen the Jewish name or the Chinese name?

HELEN No. It's wrong. Let me start again.

MILT You can't take this long, Helen. Writing a joke isn't a semiannual event.

HELEN I'm nervous. I don't know any Chinese Jews.

IRA Can I give the girl a name so I can finish this story?

CAROL Come on, give her a chance, guys.

HELEN Okay. Alright . . . I got one . . . Vito Tojo.

(They all look at her)

LUCAS Vito Tojo? . . . Vito is Italian. Tojo is Japanese.

HELEN Listen, I'm not getting paid to write this stuff.

CAROL It's alright, Helen. You got the hemispheres right.

KENNY *(To IRA)* Alright. We give up. What's his name?

IRA There's no name. It's a true story. I'm rushing back past Carnegie Hall and there's this filthy-looking bum begging on the street . . . So I give him five bucks and I start to walk away and suddenly I recognize him. It's Velvel, from Brooklyn. I went to high school with him. So I said, "Velvel, it's me. Ira Stone. Remember?" . . . And he said, "Oh, my God. Ira! How are you? What are you doing, kid?" . . . And I said, "I'm writing a big television show. For Max Prince" . . . He said, "That's great, Ira. Could you use a joke?" . . . I said, "Sure. What's the joke?" . . . He said, "It's about a Jewish girl and a Chinese man on a honeymoon. Have you heard it?" . . . I said, "No." . . . He said, "Too bad. It's a good joke. I can't remember it." . . . I felt so bad for him.

VAL   Ira, with all due respect to Velvel, what was the point in that story?

IRA   The point is, we got the breaks, he didn't. He's waiting downstairs now. I think it would be a nice gesture if we all chipped in fifty bucks apiece for Velvel. I'm giving a hundred myself. *(He points to the window)* Down there, but for the grace of God, go I.

KENNY   Well, but for the grace of God, why don't *you* go down there and send Velvel up here?

CAROL   No. I'm chipping in with Ira.

MILT   Why? You don't even know Velvel.

CAROL   I know. But every once in a while, Ira makes me cry. Go figure.

(The door opens and MAX *walks in with a drink in his hand. He is drunk)*

VAL   We were waiting for you, Max. Brian is here. Did you see Brian?

(MAX *looks dazed. He says nothing*)

BRIAN   Just dropped in from the coast to say hello, Max.

(MAX *only blinks*)

KENNY   Feeling any better, Max?

LUCAS   You want to sit down, Max? I'll get your chair.

CAROL   I wonder if he hears us?

VAL *(To MAX)*   Max! . . . It's Val . . . Can you hear what I'm saying? (MAX *looks at him*) Max, we're worried about you. *(To others)* I don't think he hears me . . .

(*They glance at each other*)

MAX   . . . Please forgive me. I'm a little drunk . . . Sometimes I don't know how to say things right . . . Maybe you never noticed . . . But as drunk as I am—I want to tell each and every person here—I love all of you! . . . Whoo! Boy! Why is that so hard to say? We never said it in my family . . . We said "eat!" . . . Eat was love. Potatoes was love. Brisket of beef was a *lot* of love . . . But Ira can tell you. I don't say it a lot.

IRA   He doesn't say it a lot.

MAX   Screw it, I'm gonna say it. I love you, I love you, I love you. Wow, does that make me hungry . . . (*He coughs*) Can everyone hear me?

LUCAS   Clear as a bell, Max.

MAX   My throat's a little sore. I was in my office and threw *up* out the window. I think I hit a little bum on the street.

IRA   That's Velvel from Brooklyn, Max. It's okay.

MAX   Oh! I have something to tell you. We *won!* . . . You hear? . . . We beat the bastards and we beat them together.

   (He starts to laugh hard; the laughter is mingled with some drunken tears)

VAL   We won what, Max? Who did we beat?

MAX   NBC! They surrendered. At five twenty-seven to-night, December twenty-fourth, nineteen hundred and—whatever . . . They signed the papers on my desk . . . It should have been on the U.S.S. *Missouri* . . . Or at Appo-mappo-mappowax! . . . We signed and we exchanged pens . . . Crappy little ballpoints they had . . . But we got what we wanted. Yessir!

KENNY   That is great news, Max.

VAL   So what was it? A new contract?

MAX   Better.

CAROL   What's better than a new contract, Max?

MAX   *Freedom!* Independence! We're out. On our own . . . From now on we call the shots.

KENNY   You mean we can go to another network? CBS?

MAX   Damn right . . . Except CBS doesn't have any air time next year. They got Walter Cronkite on everything.

BRIAN   I hear ABC is looking for new shows, Max.

MAX   There you are! ABC! . . . But they don't want to do variety. They want sports . . . What am I gonna do, play golf for an hour?

IRA   There's only three networks, Max. There's Channel Five but they've only got one camera.

MAX   Right. So what's the smartest thing we can do?

LUCAS   What?

MAX   We play the waiting game. We wait until the networks are all in trouble . . . Then they line up for us . . . with their tongues hanging out.

(The writers all look at each other)

KENNY   How long a wait are you talking about, Max?

MAX   Not long. We don't all have to wait. We break up for a while. You guys take other shows. You got families, you're in big demand, the best writers in the business . . . I'll do a couple of movies, maybe a Broadway show, play Vegas, whatever . . . and then one day the call goes out. They want us back. On our terms. The word spreads everywhere. They're getting together again. They're coming back.

MILT   Sort of like Zorro. We could wear masks and ride white horses . . . No, not white, brown.

MAX   You see? We just gotta wait 'em out . . . Maybe a year, two years, maybe ten years. We're all young. We'll only get better . . . I don't know, maybe it's a crazy idea, but it could happen if we really want it . . . What do you think?

(Silence)

IRA   You love me, I love you, Max. I'm in.

MAX   There you go.

VAL   I have a slight problem with ten years but we'll see what happens.

MAX   That's all I ask. Think about it. Don't rush. I just didn't want to say goodbye tonight . . . We're not ready for it yet . . . No goodbyes, alright?

LUCAS   I just said hello, I don't want to say goodbye.

MAX *(Nods to* LUCAS*)* . . . They didn't believe that Hannibal could cross a thousand miles over the Alps on elephants. They said the elephants would all freeze and die. And you know what Hannibal said? . . . He said, "Not if they *run* all the way." *(He breaks up laughing)* Come on. Let's celebrate. Everybody inside. Helen, go up and get my saxophone. *(*HELEN *exits)* I'm going to play "Sleighbells Roasting on an Open Fire."

*(*MAX *leaves. The others are still stunned)*

KENNY   I'll give a thousand dollars to the first one who says something intelligent.

CAROL   I think you just won it yourself.

MILT   He doesn't really mean "wait ten years," does he?

KENNY   No. It's just a metaphor.

MILT   For what?

KENNY   For "wait ten years."

VAL   I don't know what the hell to think. Somebody tell me what to think.

KENNY   Max knows it's over. And he knows *we* know it's over. But he didn't know how to say it. Not as himself. He had to become somebody else to tell us. The way he hides behind a character on the show.

BRIAN   So who was he just now?

KENNY   Hannibal! Alexander the Great! Maybe Cyclantis, whoever the hell he was.

LUCAS   Am I the only one who thinks that Max was— and don't hit me for this—astoundingly noble?

IRA   Noble? You think he was noble? He was Moses, for crise sakes. The man is a giant. He's Goliath. Maybe he's Goliath after David hit him in the head with a rock, but there's fucking greatness in him, I swear . . . He's got so much anger in him, so much pain, so much strength, so much roast beef and potato salad, that when he goes down, like he did in here tonight, with such a crash, people fell out of their beds in Belgium . . . There'll never be a Max Prince again because he's an original. I'm telling you, guys. We just lived through history.

(IRA *goes*)

KENNY Let's go in and join Moses before he eats up all the Commandments.

(*He goes*)

CAROL I can't believe it, but I think I'm going to miss speaking fuck.

MILT You're going to miss speaking it? I'm going to miss *doing* it.

BRIAN I'm telling you guys, Hollywood is great. You'll love it.

VAL Listen! If you're a Jew, you end up in the desert no matter what.

(BRIAN *laughs and they leave*)

LUCAS (*To audience*) I would have followed Max to the ends of the earth . . . But the earth went off the air on June first . . . And we all went our separate ways . . . Some up, some down, some struggled, some had more babies, and one, like Brian, died much too young . . . Helen went to law school and God knows what happened to her . . . But the most wonderful and incredible thing *did* happen . . . On the very last day of the very last show of the season, the newspapers announced that the United States Senate voted sixty-seven to twenty-two to censure Joseph McCarthy for conduct unbecoming a senator. His days were numbered ... That night Max took us all out to dinner, and he was so unbelievably funny, the tears ran down our faces, and only some of it was from laughter.

> (LUCAS *finishes his last line of dialogue to the audience. At the end we hear a lone saxophone playing* "The Christmas Song [Chestnuts Roasting on an Open Fire]" ... *eventually hitting a flat note. It keeps on playing as* MILT *comes in*)

MILT Lucas, you have to see this. Max is playing the saxophone ... and eating a corned beef sandwich at the same time.

(They look at each other)

BOTH Ba-dum-bum!

(They both leave the stage as the saxophone keeps playing)

Curtain

ABOUT THE AUTHOR

Since 1960, a Broadway season without a Neil Simon comedy or musical has been a rare one. His first play was *Come Blow Your Horn*, followed by the musical *Little Me*. During the 1966–67 season, *Barefoot in the Park*, *The Odd Couple*, *Sweet Charity*, and *The Star-Spangled Girl* were all running simultaneously; in the 1970–71 season, Broadway theatergoers had their choice of *Plaza Suite*, *Last of the Red Hot Lovers*, and *Promises, Promises*. Next came *The Gingerbread Lady*, *The Prisoner of Second Avenue*, *The Sunshine Boys*, *The Good Doctor*, *God's Favorite*, *California Suite*, *Chapter Two*, *They're Playing Our Song*, *I Ought to Be in Pictures*, *Fools*, a revival of *Little Me*, *Brighton Beach Memoirs*, *Biloxi Blues* (which won the Tony Award for Best Play), the female version of *The Odd Couple*, *Broadway Bound*, and *Rumors*. *Lost in Yonkers*, which won both the Tony Award for Best Play and the Pulitzer Prize for Drama in 1991, was followed by *Jake's Women*, the musical version of *The Goodbye Girl*, and *Laughter on the 23rd Floor*.

NEIL SIMON began his career in television, writing for *The Phil Silvers Show* and Sid Caesar's *Your Show of Shows*. Mr. Simon has also written for the screen: the adaptions of *Barefoot in the Park*, *The Odd Couple*, *Plaza Suite*, *Last of the Red Hot Lovers*, *The Prisoner of Second Avenue*, *The Sunshine Boys*, *California Suite*, *Chapter Two*, *I Ought to Be in Pictures*, *Brighton Beach Memoirs*, *Biloxi Blues*, and *Lost in Yonkers*. His other screenplays include *The Out-of-Towners*, *Murder by Death*, *The Goodbye Girl*, *The Cheap Detective*, *Seems Like Old Times*, *Only When I Laugh*, and *Max Dugan Returns*.

The author lives in California. He is married to Diane Lander and has three daughters, Ellen, Nancy, and Bryn.

From America's favorite playwright, *Laughter on the 23rd Floor* is a "screamingly funny" (*Philadelphia Inquirer*) Broadway hit about a team of comedy writers in television's Golden Age.

Set in 1953, Neil Simon's "flat-out funniest play in years" (Dennis Cunningham, CBS-TV) re-creates the mayhem, neuroses, nonstop gags, and constant one-upmanship of a team of brilliantly funny social misfits as they write *The Max Prince Show,* a weekly variety program. Among the crew are Milt, the insult artist; Ira, the hypochondriac whose dream is to have a virus named after him; and Val, a Russian emigré who takes a Berlitz course so he can curse without an accent. They are devoted to their boss, Max, a comic genius, a tyrant, and a paranoiac with a heart of gold. But his penchant for tippling and popping too many pills is growing under the pressures of a rising McCarthyism, network executives, and sponsors who want him to cut back his "too-smart" show and staff so that they can chase after the *Leave It to Beaver* and *Father Knows Best* audience.

Broadway's funniest playwright writing about a team of comedy writers? It's no wonder *Laughter on the 23rd Floor* is "the funniest comedy on Broadway in years" (*Variety*).